God's World from a Child's Point of View

LITTLE MINDS WITH BIG HEARTS

God's World from a Child's Point of View

LITTLE MINDS WITH BIG HEARTS

Compiled by

RAMONA CRAMER TUCKER
Editor of *Today's Christian Woman*

MOODY PRESS
CHICAGO

ISBN: 0-8024-4777-5

1 3 5 7 9 10 8 6 4 2

Printed in the United States of America

Contents

INTRODUCTION

Oh, the funny things kids say! Children can be a trove of heartwarming quips and quotes. So whether you're a parent, teacher, grandparent, youth worker, or just someone who enjoys being around children, when you have a "little one" in your life, your days are filled with the blessing of unexpected humor.

This book, *Little Minds with Big Hearts*, features 400 warm and witty stories from kids or about kids—the best "small talk" culled from five years of "Heart to Heart" entries from *Today's Christian Woman* magazine. Collected from families across the country, these "little lessons" will make you laugh. A few will make you cry. But all will encourage you in your day-to-day life.

Whether you read through this book in a single sitting or pick it up in leisurely moments when you're in need of a good chuckle, you'll enjoy reading children's interpretations of:

- BIBLE BASICS
- PITHY PRAYERS
- SCHOOL DAYS
- CHURCH HAPPENINGS
- SPECIAL SONGS
- FOOD AND FAMILY
- GOD AND HEAVEN
- HOLIDAY MOMENTS AND MUCH, MUCH MORE!

Who knows? Maybe after reading *Little Minds with Big Hearts*, you'll want to start a "family journal" of your own favorite tales from your tots!

Bible Basics

FOR THE RECORD

One morning my four young children and I were reviewing what God did on each of the seven days of creation. When we got to the seventh day, my youngest raised his hand frantically and yelled, "I know, Mom. I know. On the seventh day, God got arrested!"

Kay White, California

For you are the Fountain of life; our light is from your Light.

Psalm 36:9 TLB

STICKY WEALTH

While I was reading a Bible story to my children about the influence Jesus had on Zacchaeus, my daughter wanted to know just how rich Zacchaeus was. I tried to explain with descriptions of how his home, chariot, and clothes may have looked, but nothing seemed to impress her. Then her older brother piped up. "He was so rich he had enough money to buy one hundred pieces of gum!" With that explanation her eyes lit up, and the enormity of Zacchaeus's wealth and what he did with it for Jesus sank in.

Lisa Arnold, Pennsylvania

Those who have reason to be thankful should continually be singing praises to the Lord.

James 5:13 TLB

LITTLE LOTTO

When the four children I watched fought over who got to take the lint off the screen on the dryer, pour soap in the washer, or push the button down on the toaster, I would make them pick a number between one and ten. Later, when I was teaching them the story of David and Goliath and trying to emphasize how David did not need to earn God's favor for God to choose him to do His special job, three-year-old Stevie looked at me with sudden understanding and said, "Oh—David just picked the right number."

Deana Galang, California

If anyone obeys his word, God's love is truly made complete in him.

1 John 2:5

UH-OH!

During the Saturday evening service at our church, my husband and I were teaching a Bible lesson to the three and four year olds. Before asking the blessing for our snack, I asked, "Does anyone know what Jesus said to His disciples when He broke the bread?" A little voice proclaimed, "Uh-oh!"

Terrie Rodgers, Indiana

Anyone who believes in me already has eternal life! Yes, I am the Bread of Life!

John 6:47–48 TLB

MINIATURE THEOLOGIAN

When our son Daniel disobeyed us, we'd send him to his room to "think about what he had done" for a while. Then we'd go in and talk with him. On one occasion, Daniel was sitting on his bed, looking mournful. When asked why he had done wrong, he replied, "But Mommy, sometimes I feel there's a good guy sitting on one side of me and a bad guy on the other, telling me to do different things. And this time the good guy was late!"

Bobbie Zimmerman, Minnesota

He heals the brokenhearted, binding up their wounds. . . . The Lord supports the humble. . . .

Psalm 147:3, 6 TLB

IMPORTANT GUEST

While telling my eight-year-old cousin that Jesus Christ wants to be a part of his life, I read to him Revelation 3:20: "Here I am! I stand at the door and knock. If anyone hears my voice and opens the door, I will come in and eat with him, and he with me." As I began to explain the verse, there was a knock on the bedroom door. My cousin jumped up and down excitedly and yelled, "Quick, open it! Jesus is here!"

Rachel Thomas, Saudi Arabia

Wait for the Lord; be strong and take heart and wait for the Lord.

Psalm 27:14

PARTNERS

My three-year-old daughter, Karlin, and I were reading a toddler version of the Bible story about Moses speaking with God as He appeared in a pillar of cloud. Afterward, I asked Karlin some simple questions that she answered correctly. Then I asked who was talking with Moses. Obviously somewhat confused, Karlin replied, "Jesus and . . ." After a long pause, she added, "Who is that other guy He works with?"

Karen Lyall, Oklahoma

Jesus Christ is the same yesterday and today and forever.

Hebrews 13:8

A VERY SPECIAL GARDEN

My family and I were playing Bible Trivia, and the youngest player was my three-and-a-half-year-old niece, Kristen (who is also an avid gardener, like her mother). My sister, Vickie, was master of ceremonies for the game and was quickly perusing the questions, trying to find a simple one that Kristen could answer. "OK, Kristen, this one's for you," Vickie announced. We all braced ourselves for the simplest Bible question in the history of trivia. Instead, Vickie asked, "What did Jesus do in the Garden of Gethsemane?" Kristen looked around with big, round blue eyes and answered simply, "He watered the flowers."

Debbie Andreasen, Illinois

Perseverance must finish its work so that you may be mature and complete, not lacking anything.

James 1:4

OH, BROTHER!

After I read a Bible story to my children, my four-year-old son looked up at me and said, "You know, we hear lots of things about God, but this is the first story I've heard about His brother, Lord."

Charlene Kay Heim, Kansas

I am the Living One; I was dead, and behold I am alive for ever and ever!

Revelation 1:18

SOUNDS LIKE POPEYE

When my son was four years old, our family watched *The Ten Commandments.* When it came to the part where God's voice comes from the burning bush saying, "Tell them, I Am that I Am has sent you," my son turned to me and said, "Hey, God is Popeye!"

Phyllis Wilson, Louisiana

The Lord will send a blessing on your barns and on everything you put your hand to. The Lord your God will bless you in the land he is giving you.

Deuteronomy 28:8

NIGHT-LITE READING

Because of my hectic schedule, I usually have my devotions at night. One evening while I was reading my Bible, my three-year-old son came into my bedroom with one of his favorite bedtime stories for me to read. When he saw what I was reading, he said, "You're not going to read that whole book tonight, are you, Mom?"

Cheryl S. Bellocq, Louisiana

God . . . has blessed us with every blessing in heaven because we belong to Christ.

Ephesians 1:3 TLB

EXTRA CREDIT

While putting my four year old to bed, I read her the story of the Prodigal Son. We discussed how the young son had taken his inheritance and left home, living it up until he had nothing left. Finally, when he couldn't even eat as well as pigs, he went home to his father, who welcomed him. When we finished the story, I asked my daughter what she had learned. After thinking a moment, she quipped, "Never leave home without your credit card!"

Jolene Horn, California

You have made known to me the paths of life; you will fill me with joy in your presence.

Acts 2:28

THE ELEVENTH COMMANDMENT

One morning when my son was four, he came into my room looking very confused. Through sleepy eyes I could see he was holding his Bible and trying to read it. I asked him what was wrong. Nothing could have prepared me for his reply: "Mom, I want you to show me in this Bible where it says I can't run in the house."

Shelley Telfer, Oregon

As for me and my household, we will serve the Lord.
Joshua 24:15

PROMISES, PROMISES

It was late winter, and during the night it had snowed four or five inches—an unusual amount for our part of the country. My youngest daughter, who had never seen snow before, came running into our bedroom, upset. "Mother, Mother!" she exclaimed. "You told us God said He'd never drown the world in a flood again, and now look what He's done!"

Phyllis Haughton, Virginia

He is my refuge and my fortress, my God, in whom I trust.
Psalm 91:2

PET PREFERENCE

While wrapping up devotions with my four-year-old daughter, Tori, I quizzed her on the lesson. My last question for her was: "Why do you think God preferred Abel's gift to Cain's?" Without a moment's hesitation, she sighed. "Oh, Mommy, that's easy! God liked Abel's gift because he gave Him a pet and all Cain gave Him was something to eat!"

Shawntel Allen, West Africa

Those of us who reverence the Lord will never lack any good thing.

Psalm 34:10 TLB

FISHY TALE

On the way to church, my nephew, Danny, was listening to a Bible tape. It was the story about Jesus feeding thousands of people with a few fish and loaves. His mom commented, "Danny, isn't it a miracle Jesus could feed all those people?" He thought a moment and replied, "I just want to know . . . just how big were those fish?"

Carol Rose, Oregon

My word that goes out from my mouth: It will not return to me empty, but will accomplish what I desire and achieve the purpose for which I sent it.

Isaiah 55:11

FIERY FRACAS

After reading a bedtime Bible story about the three men in the fiery furnace, I asked my five-year-old daughter, Emily, if she could remember the names of the three men. She thought, then confidently counted off, "Shadrach, Meshach, and Cataract!"

Shelly Rankin, Illinois

You have given me your salvation as my shield. Your right hand, O Lord, supports me; your gentleness has made me great.

Psalm 18:35 TLB

FLOOD TRIVIA

When my niece, Cassi, was five, we were playing Bible Trivia with her family. Her question was, "What did the Lord tell Noah to build before the Flood came?" She was quite pleased with herself as she blurted out her answer, "He build-ed an aardvark!"

Peg Magnuson, Minnesota

The Lord loves us. He will bring us safely into the land and give it to us.

Numbers 14:8 TLB

A KINDER PUNISHMENT

While riding in the car with my four-year-old Fraser, I told him that Jesus loved him so much He was beaten and hanged on a cross to die as the punishment for all the bad things we do. Fraser pondered this. Then he said thoughtfully, "Wouldn't it have been easier if they had just given Him a spanking, Mommy?"

Michelle Stewart, Ontario

Everyone who believes in him may have eternal life.

John 3:15

SHOUTING THE COMMANDMENTS

My four-year-old niece, Amanda, and I were taking a walk when we saw some pretty flowers she wanted to pick. I explained that we couldn't pick them because it would be stealing. Then I asked her, "What does stealing mean?" She replied by yelling, "THOU SHOUT NOT STEAL!" Not understanding why she yelled, I asked her again. Once more she yelled, "Thou SHOUT not steal!"

Katie Payne, New York

If you make the Most High your dwelling—even the Lord, who is my refuge—then no harm will befall you.

Psalm 91:9–10

SALT AND PEPPER

Recently my six year old, Katelyn, was watching Christian cartoons on television. After the program was over, she began discussing the story of Sodom and Gomorrah with her older sister. When she came to the part when Lot's wife turned into a pillar of salt, she added, "And he probably turned into pepper!"

Joni McClintock, Oregon

God will judge us for everything we do, including every hidden thing, good or bad.

Ecclesiastes 12:14 TLB

A TWISTED COMMANDMENT

My husband and I start weekdays with a half hour of family devotions before the children head off to school. One morning while discussing the Ten Commandments, we asked the kids if they could name them all. They mentioned the usual ones: "Thou shalt not kill . . . thou shalt not steal," and so on. Then our eleven year old chimed in with, "Thou shalt not admit adultery to your neighbor's wife." Obviously we had some clarifying to do.

Eric and Jayne Post, California

Give ear and come to me; hear me, that your soul may live. I will make an everlasting covenant with you, my faithful love promised to David.

Isaiah 55:3

QUICK MATH

I was driving to work one morning with my four year old when she remarked, "Mommy, you know what? I know everything there is to know." "Really?" I said. "If you know everything there is to know, then what is two times two?" She quickly answered, "I know—that's the way the animals came on the ark—two times two!"

Sheri Brumit, Maryland

It is good both to hope and wait quietly for the salvation of the Lord.

Lamentations 3:26 TLB

ELISHA MEETS M. J.

My son's Sunday school teacher was telling the story of Naaman, the leper who was healed after dipping in the Jordan River seven times according to Elisha's instructions. Near the end of class, she noticed that Matthew was daydreaming and asked him to recap the story. After thinking for a moment, he confidently replied, "Elisha told Michael Jordan to go slam-dunk seven times beside the river."

Debbie Coty, Florida

Everyone who asks receives; he who seeks finds; and to him who knocks, the door will be opened.

Luke 11:10

PERFECT PENMANSHIP

While sitting next to my first-grade daughter during the morning worship service, I noticed her looking at my open Bible. In a whisper, she asked, "Did God really write that?" "Yes," I whispered back. Looking down at the Bible again, she said in amazement, "Wow! He really has neat handwriting!"

Susan Wright, Florida

Many blessings are given to those who trust the Lord.

Psalm 40:4 TLB

Pithy Prayers

FRUIT OF THE SPIRIT

During lunchtime at school, an especially difficult child turned and called my name. "Miss Maria," he said, "we forgot to save our pears!" He had just eaten his helping of mixed fruit, so I halfheartedly told him he could eat his fruit however he wanted to. Again he insisted, "But we forgot to save our pears!" I was ready to forget the entire conversation when I realized he'd been saying, "We forgot to say our prayers!"

Maria Johnson, Michigan

Let us press on to know him, and he will respond to us as surely as the coming of dawn or the rain of early spring.

Hosea 6:3 TLB

DIVINE DIRECTION

One day I decided to take my three children to an ice skating party in a nearby town, but after several wrong turns and stops to ask directions, I pulled over to the side of the road and suggested we all ask God to help us find the rink. When we finally arrived, we were nearly an hour late. The following week as we got into the car to go skating again, my five-year-old son exclaimed, "Mom, let's pray now and save time!"

Pegi Tehan, Ohio

Commit everything you do to the Lord. Trust him to help you do it and he will.

Psalm 37:5 TLB

QUICK LEARNER

My two year old was accustomed to our family's tradition of praying before meals. One evening while I was cooking, he appeared in the kitchen and announced he was ready for supper. "It's not time to eat yet," I told him. Immediately he walked over to the table, crawled into his booster seat, and proclaimed, "AMEN!" Then he asked me, "Can I eat now?"

Tambi Swiney, Tennessee

Give thanks to the Lord for his unfailing love and his wonderful deeds for men, for he satisfies the thirsty and fills the hungry with good things.

Psalm 107:8–9

A WORD TO THE WISE

When my daughter was four, I tried to teach her that God sent His Son to die so that we could be forgiven of our sins. I wasn't sure if I had explained this to her very well, so I was pleased when she wanted to initiate her own prayer. "Dear Jesus," she began, "thank You for giving us our sins. Amen!"

Bambi L. Kelly, Texas

We fix our eyes not on what is seen, but on what is unseen. For what is seen is temporary, but what is unseen is eternal.

2 Corinthians 4:18

THE BREAD OF LIFE

While baby-sitting some children from another family, I asked each of them to take turns asking the blessing at meal-times. The difference in our family prayer styles didn't go unnoticed by my five-year-old daughter. The next morning at breakfast, she bowed her head and proceeded to pray, "Thank You, Father, Son, and Holy Toast!"

Sandra Giffin, Missouri

Ask, and you will be given what you ask for. Seek, and you will find. Knock, and the door will be opened.

Matthew 7:7 TLB

WHICH MARY?

My two year old, Caleb, recently showed us how much he understood about Jesus' life. One evening while my husband picked up our new baby-sitter, I explained to Caleb that while we were gone, his baby-sitter, Mary, would be staying with him. Caleb turned, rather surprised, and asked, "Jesus too?"

Valerie Miller, Washington

He will keep in perfect peace all those who trust in him, whose thoughts turn often to the Lord!

Isaiah 26:3 TLB

SPECIAL REQUEST

Our church was having a week of prayer services. As I was getting ready to go one evening, my granddaughter asked me to stay home with her. I attempted to appease her by telling her I'd try to be home early. "Nan," she said, pouting, "could you please just pray a little faster tonight?"

Gladys Noble, Newfoundland

You will seek me and find me when you seek me with all your heart.

Jeremiah 29:13

PLEASE, MR. PLEASE

I was reading my almost-three-year-old daughter, Andrea, the story of the Israelites asking Samuel to ask God for a king. When I said to her, "How do you ask God for something?" I was trying to elicit the answer "Pray." Instead, she immediately responded, "May I please have king?"

Karen M. Stevenson, Virginia

Whatever is true, whatever is noble, whatever is right, whatever is pure, whatever is lovely, whatever is admirable—if anything is excellent or praiseworthy—think about such things.

Philippians 4:8

TIME OUT

My three-year-old grandson, Tyson, was beginning to grasp the idea of asking Jesus for help. When he was in his car seat, he heard my sister, Julie, whom he lovingly calls "Jewel Baby," cough. "Are you sick, Jewel Baby?" he asked. "Yes," she responded. He promptly prayed, "Sick, get off Jewel Baby and go to Time Out. In Jesus' name, Amen."

Donna R. James, California

Whoever finds his life will lose it, and whoever loses his life for my sake will find it.

Matthew 10:39

LIBERTY AND JUSTICE FOR ALL

One evening I stopped by a friend's house and caught her in bedtime procedures. "Come on in," she insisted. "You can join us for prayers." After tucking the covers around her six-year-old daughter, she asked, "What would you like to pray for tonight?" "Liberty and Justice," Taylor replied. My friend glowed with maternal pride. "Honey, what do you know about liberty and justice?" "Oh," Taylor answered, "They're Jennifer's dogs."

Rhonda Reese, Florida

Keep putting into practice all you learned from me and saw me doing, and the God of peace will be with you.

Philippians 4:9 TLB

SMALL TALK

One day our oldest daughter, Ashleigh, asked her two-year-old sister, Kaitlyn, to pray for her because she didn't feel well. Kaitlyn took Ashleigh's hand and prayed earnestly, "Jesus, Ashleigh." That was it. Her two simple words reminded me what Jesus meant when He said we should have child-like faith. I don't need eloquent words to be heard by my heavenly Father—just communication from my heart.

Lynette Kittle, Florida

For as high as the heavens are above the earth, so great is his love for those who fear him.

Psalm 103:11

JOURNEYING MERCIES

A co-worker was teaching our preschoolers about how Jesus would someday return and take us home with Him. As we started prayer time later that afternoon, we had to smile as one little girl prayed for Jesus to have a "safe trip back."

Darlene M. Grieco, Pennsylvania

The Lord God is my Strength, and he will give me the speed of a deer and bring me safely over the mountains.

Habakkuk 3:19 TLB

SIDETRACKED

My husband and I often tell our children not to get sidetracked from things we've asked them to do around the house. One night I was praying with four-year-old Aaron while his father and older sister were at the Saturday night worship service. He said, "Mom, are you sure God won't get sidetracked from the church service if we talk to Him at the same time?"

Susanne Badilla, Alaska

The righteous will flourish like a palm tree, they will grow like a cedar of Lebanon; planted in the house of the Lord.

Psalm 92:12–13

ADVANCE THANKS

Our three-year-old grandson, Kyle, was playing in his wading pool when he said, "Momma, don't we have a lot of nice toys? Let's thank God for our nice toys." After Kyle and his mother prayed together, he was quiet for a while, then grinned. "Maybe if we say thank You, God, for our Nintendo game, He'll get us one!"

Kathryn K. Butcher, Michigan

Do not be anxious about anything, but in everything, by prayer and petition, with thanksgiving, present your requests to God.

Philippians 4:6

A PLATEFUL OF PRAYER?

Our three-year-old grandson, Daniel, stayed with us while his parents went on a trip. As usual, we bowed our heads as my husband prayed out loud before all our meals. Daniel watched curiously each time Grandpa prayed. On the day his parents came to pick him up, we all sat down at the table to have lunch. Just as his daddy started to pick up his sandwich, Daniel shouted, "Wait, Daddy, we can't eat till Grandpa reads his plate!"

Diana L. James, California

Be encouraged and knit together by strong ties of love, and . . . you will have the rich experience of knowing Christ with real certainty and clear understanding.

Colossians 2:2 TLB

LETTUCE TALK

It was our three-year-old daughter's turn to ask the blessing over the evening meal. Sarah began. "God is great. God is good. Let us thank . . . " At that point she looked at her daddy, pointed to his tossed salad, and said, "Look, Dad, there's the let us."

Mary H. Simpson, Kentucky

Humble yourselves before the Lord, and he will lift you up.

James 4:10

A DIFFERENT KIND OF AMEN

One Sunday afternoon we were visiting my parents with our two-year-old son, Justin. After lunch, Grampa read from the Bible and prayed. When he was done, we waited for a reverent "amen" from Justin, but instead we heard a cheery, "That's all, folks!"

Willette Swanson, British Columbia

When I pray, you answer me, and encourage me by giving me the strength I need.

Psalm 138:3 TLB

AND GOD BLESS . . .

My three year old kneeled by her bed to say her prayers before going to sleep. "God bless Mommie, God bless Daddy, God bless my brother Doug, God bless my cousin Bruce . . ." As I sat listening, she finished by looking skyward and saying enthusiastically, "And God bless You too, God!"

Virginia Kelly Homan, Colorado

The Lord upholds all those who fall and lifts up all who are bowed down.

Psalm 145:14

DO IT YOURSELF PRAYER

My daughter, Sarah, was four when she got the stomach flu. Every few minutes we'd race for the bathroom. I was holding a cold cloth to her head and trying to speak comforting words when she asked, "Mommy, would you pray for me?" So I offered a short prayer. Within minutes, she was sick again. Once we got her cleaned up, she looked me squarely in the eye and pronounced, "I'll pray for myself next time."

Pam Lebo, Maryland

In my great trouble I cried to the Lord and he answered me; from the depths of death I called, and Lord, you heard me!

Jonah 2:2 TLB

GOD ON CALL

Our three-year-old nephew, Robbie, and his family were preparing to leave for their trip home from Grandma's house. His mom prayed for a safe trip, then Robbie prayed, "Dear God, please get us home safely. And if we get in an accident, please call 911 fast! Amen!"

Carrie Duwe, Washington

The Lord is my light and my salvation—whom shall I fear? The Lord is the stronghold of my life—of whom shall I be afraid?

Psalm 27:1

HOWARD BE THY FATHER

My husband had been teaching our four-year-old son the Lord's Prayer. Finally, Michael wanted to say it by himself. I walked into the room just as he began, "Our Father, who art in heaven, Howard be my name . . ."

Fran Severance, California

God has chosen poor people to be rich in faith, and the Kingdom of Heaven is theirs, for that is the gift God has promised to all those who love him.

James 2:5 TLB

CUSTOMER SERVICE

When my nephew Jordan asked his mom for a "Nerf" bow and arrow, she told him he should pray about it. They sat down, and she prayed that God would provide good toys for Jordan. About an hour later, he ran back to his mom and in his three-year-old voice inquired, "So what did He say?"

Kimberly Noel, Florida

The word of the Lord is right and true; he is faithful in all he does.

Psalm 33:4

SCHOOL DAZE

CONVOLUTED VERSION

Partway through the school year, I had managed to teach my preschoolers the Lord's Prayer. One day a three year old volunteered to lead it for the class: "Our Father, who artist in heaven, Halloween be Your name. Thy Kingdom come, Thy will be done, one nation under God, invisible, with livery for all. Amen."

Denise Koetje, Michigan

All these blessings will come upon you and accompany you if you obey the Lord your God: . . . The fruit of your womb will be blessed, and the crops of your land.

Deuteronomy 28:2, 4

GOD IN MY SHOES

One afternoon I arrived at the preschool where my daughter works and my two-and-a-half-year-old granddaughter, Nina, attends. The teacher had just led the children in prayer, and now my daughter eagerly coaxed Nina to "tell Nana about Jesus and where He is." Nina shyly smiled, bent her head down, and said in a soft whisper, "Jesus is in my heart." As we digested this profession of faith from this small innocent voice, we were startled to hear "And He's in my shoes too!"

Bitsy (Nana) Craft, Indiana

And whoever welcomes a little child like this in my name welcomes me.

Matthew 18:5

SUBSTITUTE STORY

Lacing up my hiking boots before taking my eight-year-old Jeff to school, I noticed he looked confused by my casual dress—he knew I was going to work. I explained, "We get to wear whatever we want this week, because the bosses are out of town." He considered this a moment, then asked, "Will you have a substitute?"

Joyce A. Davis, Georgia

Love one another. As I have loved you, so you must love one another.

John 13:34

LAST ISN'T THE END

My eight year old was in her bedroom doing homework one evening. She came out agitated and complaining about having to answer the question, "How did you celebrate your last birthday?" She was near tears as she voiced her frustration. "Mommy, how can I tell my teacher how I celebrated my last birthday when I'm not even in my twenties?"

Ginger Reed, Ohio

The Lord is my fort where I can enter and be safe. . . . He is a rugged mountain where I hide; he is my Savior, a rock where none can reach me, and a tower of safety.

Psalm 18:2 TLB

CREDIT CONFUSION

One day my six-year-old nephew came home from kindergarten and told his mother he was mad at her for not teaching him how to spell his last name. He said that, if he'd known how, he could have gotten money at school. Puzzled, his mother asked him to explain, and he did: "My teacher said if we could spell our last name she would give us credit."

Jan Artrip, Iowa

For if you give, you will get! Your gift will return to you in full and overflowing measure, pressed down, shaken together to make room for more, and running over.

Luke 6:38 TLB

HEARTS GALORE

On the way to preschool one morning, my four-year-old daughter, Landen, said, "Mommy, did you know that when we get to heaven Jesus is going to take away our old hearts and give us a new heart?" When I nodded yes, she paused, then said, "I don't know what He will do with all the old ones . . . I guess He'll just sit on them!"

Beth Ellis, Texas

The Lord will fulfill [his purpose] for me; your love, O Lord, endures forever.

Psalm 138:8

THE GOLDEN RULE

My son's first-grade teacher challenged her class to live the Golden Rule for one week. Later that week she sent Tymon and his classmate Bobby to the principal's office to be disciplined for fighting. When the principal asked why he had hit Bobby, Tymon responded, "I done him the Golden Rule." Puzzled, the principal asked him to explain. Innocently Tymon replied, "Bobby hit me, so I hit him back."

Linda LaMar Jewell, New Mexico

Only the Lord knows! He searches all hearts and examines deepest motives so he can give to each person his right reward, according to his deeds—how he has lived.

Jeremiah 17:10 TLB

WHOSE BIRTHDAY?

When my daughter, Megan, was in nursery school, I convinced her teacher to have the class make harvest crafts for Halloween instead of witches and ghosts. But when Christmas came, I knew Santa would be visiting their room, and the children were excited about it. I asked Megan, "What will you tell Santa when you sit on his lap and give him your list?" Megan replied smartly, "I tell Santa it's Jesus' birthday."

JoAnne I. Wood, Connecticut

Though he [Jehovah] is so great, he respects the humble.

Psalm 138:6 TLB

FUN, FUN, FUN

When my first graders were coloring angels for a bulletin board, I noticed they were all coloring the angels' hair pale yellow. I asked, "Why are you all coloring the angels' hair blonde?" One brave little girl raised her hand and explained, "Teacher, don't you know blondes have more fun?"

Bonnie S. Baumgardner, North Carolina

Always be full of joy in the Lord; I say it again, rejoice!
Philippians 4:4 TLB

U TURN

While running errands one afternoon, I inadvertently rushed past the street where I needed to make a left turn. I thought aloud, "I wonder if I can make a U at this corner?" My kindergartner, Jodi, calmly suggested, "Mommy, why don't you make a lowercase E?"

Lou Ann Noren, California

In all these things we are more than conquerors through him who loved us.
Romans 8:37

SKY-HIGH RECYCLING

One day during a day-care field trip, my daughter Hayley and her classmates each received a balloon. But as they were loading into the van to go home, Hayley's balloon flew away. One sincerely disappointed boy asked the teacher, "Mrs. Couch, what will happen to Hayley's balloon?" Another little boy confidently responded, "Don't worry—God will give it to someone up there!"

Bambi Dossey, Texas

Blessings on all who reverence and trust the Lord—on all who obey him! Their reward shall be prosperity and happiness.

Psalm 128:1–2 TLB

SPEED READER

During a January writing lesson, I asked my third graders to record their New Year's resolutions in their journals. I said that one of mine was to read the Bible daily during my morning quiet time. One wide-eyed boy looked at me doubtfully and exclaimed, "How can you possibly do that? It took my mom a year to read the Bible!"

Julie Trout, Missouri

I will give you one heart and a new spirit; I will take from you your hearts of stone and give you tender hearts of love for God.

Ezekiel 11:19 TLB

THE LAST SHALL BE FIRST

As a preschool teacher I frequently deal with the "me first" syndrome. I try to dispel the problem biblically by teaching the children Jesus' command about serving others first. It seems to sink in—the students start taking turns and letting others go ahead in games. But one day, during a game, the last two children to take their turns both offered to go last. Finally one protested strongly, "But I asked to go last first!"

Susan Blair, Georgia

I can do everything through him who gives me strength.

Philippians 4:13

HEADACHES AND HEARTACHES

My four-year-old twins, Luke and Benjamin, are great friends. As they started preschool, I worried about the first time one would have to attend without the other due to illness. That day finally came. I explained to Ben that Luke's head hurt, so he couldn't go to school. Then I prayed with him that the Lord would give him a great day. After we prayed, Ben looked up at me and with great empathy said, "I can't go to school today either, Mom. My feelings hurt."

Missy Gertz, Hawaii

"For I know the plans I have for you," declares the Lord, "plans to prosper you and not to harm you, plans to give you hope and a future."

Jeremiah 29:11

Special Songs

PRICKLY PEAS

My three-year-old son, J.J., loves to sing. One day he was listening to a tape, and instead of singing, "Prince of Peace, Mighty God, Holy One," J.J. belted out, "Prickly Pea, Spiny God, Only One!"

Julie Taylor, Ohio

If God is on our side, who can ever be against us?

Romans 8:31 TLB

A NO-BRAINER

One afternoon our five year old, Katie, was singing a Scripture song we had recently learned. While my husband and I listened proudly, she came to a verse about becoming blameless. Katie confidently sang out, "Do everything without arguing, so that you may become brainless and pure, children of God."

Lynn Hall, Wyoming

The Lord will guide you continually, and satisfy you with all good things, and keep you healthy too.

Isaiah 58:11 TLB

GRIN AND BEAR IT

A friend of mine used to teach Sunday school, and her favorite hymn to sing in class was "Oh, the Consecrated Cross I Bear." One Sunday a concerned mother questioned my friend about a song her child said she'd learned in class. Her daughter had been singing, "Oh, the constipated, cross-eyed bear!"

Kirsten Jackson, Oklahoma

May the God of peace himself make you entirely pure and devoted to God. . . . God, who called you to become his child, will do all this for you, just as he promised.

1 Thessalonians 5:23–24 TLB

GOATS TELL IT ON THE MOUNTAIN

My three-year-old son, Grant, told me he learned a new song in children's church about goats on the mountain when Jesus was born. I hadn't heard that one before, so I asked him to sing it. He began. "Goats tell it on the mountain, over the hills and everywhere. Goats tell it on the mountain, that Jesus Christ is born."

Debbie Harmon, Kansas

We wait in hope for the Lord; he is our help and our shield.

Psalm 33:20

PRETTY CHEESY

My three-year-old great-grandson was in church with me as we sang the old favorite "Bringing in the sheaves, bringing in the sheaves, we will come rejoicing bringing in the sheaves." After the song, he tugged at my hand and whispered loudly, "Grandma, what's God going to do with all that cheese?"

Ardith Thiel, Minnesota

He has showered down upon us the richness of his grace—for how well he understands us and knows what is best for us at all times.

Ephesians 1:8 TLB

SOUNDING OFF

One morning my three year old, Katherine, reminded me that God wants me to come to Him just as I am. She was singing and dancing around the house as usual, but as I listened, I noticed she was singing, "I love you, Lord, and I lift my noise!"

Sandra James, California

Look! I have been standing at the door and I am constantly knocking. If anyone hears me calling him and opens the door, I will come in and fellowship with him and he with me.

Revelation 3:20 TLB

VARIATION ON A THEME

On Palm Sunday, my five-year-old niece, Stephanie, sat on my lap while we listened to the pastor's sermon. He described Jesus' approach to Jerusalem and how the crowds cried, "Hosanna, Hosanna!" At that, Stephanie perked up and began to sing, "Oh, Hosanna, now don't you cry for me!"

Brenda Fossum, Minnesota

Their Redeemer is strong. His name is the Lord of Hosts. He will plead for them and see that they are freed to live again in quietness.

Jeremiah 50:34 TLB

DINGDONG PRAISE

My four year old, Joshua, loves to sing with me. I always get a chuckle when we sing the praise chorus "Majesty." Joshua's version begins, "Majesty, ding-dong authority . . ."

Carmon S. Ellis, Michigan

Keep traveling steadily along his pathway and in due season he will honor you with every blessing.

Psalm 37:34 TLB

HOLY DIAPERS

While traveling in the car, my three-year-old daughter, Hannah, and I were singing along with our tape of "Jesus Loves the Little Children." Upon hearing the second verse—which begins "Jesus died for all the children"—Hannah looked at me with surprise and asked, "Jesus diapers all the children? Yuck!"

Marcella Koenig, Indiana

We are already God's children, right now, and we can't even imagine what it is going to be like later on. But we do know this, that when he comes we will be like him, as a result of seeing him as he really is.

1 John 3:2 TLB

HOME ON THE RANGE?

While we sat around a campfire one night, my four-year-old daughter, Kelsey, began to sing a familiar tune, "Home on the Range." But her version was somewhat different: "Oh, Home on the Range, where the deer and the ants all go play."

Lisa Skaggs, Ohio

May the God who gives endurance and encouragement give you a spirit of unity among yourselves as you follow Christ Jesus.

Romans 15:5

JOY TO THE WORLD

One summer day I was baby-sitting four children down the street. They were busily playing in their front yard when three-year-old Erin stood on a big rock and started singing, "Joy to the world, the Lord has fun!"

Robin Oppenhuizen, Michigan

Believe God! It will be just as he said!

Acts 27:25 TLB

THE B-I-B-L-E

At age two, our daughter was already singing Sunday school songs for us. She inspired peals of laughter when one morning she teetered into the kitchen hauling the biggest Bible in the house. She placed the Bible on the floor and stepped up on it. Smiling from ear to ear she sang, "The B-I-B-L-E, yes, that's the book for me. I stand alone on the Word of God, the B-I-B-L-E."

Melissa B. Clarke, Pennsylvania

When I am afraid, I will put my confidence in you. Yes, I will trust the promises of God. And since I am trusting him, what can mere man do to me?

Psalm 56:3–4 TLB

ANIMAL ACTIVIST

My husband was holding our two year old during the worship time at church. As we all sang, "Worthy is the Lamb," she let out a loud "BAAAAA!"

Margaret M. Cuomo, New York

The Lord has declared today that you are his very own people, just as he promised.

Deuteronomy 26:18 TLB

SING IT AGAIN, JAMES

After an exciting Christmas season, our four year old, James, was reliving it all by singing Christmas songs. I was surprised when he began to sing "Hark, the Herald Angels Sing" with slightly different lyrics: "Hark, there goes the angel singing, 'Thank you for the newborn King . . .' "

Barbara M. Heard, Virginia

For God so loved the world that he gave his one and only Son, that whoever believes in him shall not perish but have eternal life.

John 3:16

BIRD EGGS AT YOUR FEET

When my daughter, Theresa, was three years old, one of her favorite songs was "I Cast All My Cares." One day as I listened to her sweet rendition, I heard her sing, "I'll cast all my cares upon You . . . I'll lay all of my bird eggs down at Your feet." I guess, to a three year old, bird eggs are more real than burdens.

Susanne Badilla, Alaska

Your faithfulness extends to every generation, like the earth you created; it endures by your decree, for everything serves your plans.

Psalm 119:90–91 TLB

HALLELUJAH CRAZIES

At night as he's trying to fall asleep, my son sometimes sings songs he's learned in Sunday school. Since he's not yet able to use his *l*'s, we were greatly amused to hear him sing, "Ha-way-woo, ha-way-woo, ha-way-woo, ha-way-woo-yah! Cwazy do Woord!"

Sharon Higgins, Minnesota

He will hold you aloft in his hands for all to see—a splendid crown for the King of kings.

Isaiah 62:3 TLB

I GOT BRAINS!

During a musical celebration at church, my three year old, Kyle, was getting into the spirit of things when we began to sing a familiar chorus: "Our God reigns . . . Hallelujah . . . Our God reigns." Kyle joined in, "I got brains . . . Hallelujah . . . I got brains!" He got a good laugh from at least three rows around us.

Lisa Skaggs, Ohio

I am sending Christ to be the carefully chosen, precious Cornerstone of my church, and I will never disappoint those who trust in him.

1 Peter 2:6 TLB

Name Game

HIGH HOPES

Our family gathered in the living room one fall evening. Feeling a little chilled, I asked my three-year-old daughter, Jada, to shut the front door so the draft wouldn't come in. Looking excited, she ran to the door. A few moments later, she peeked around the corner and said in a disappointed tone, "Mommy, I don't see a giraffe!"

Christy Duncan, Texas

Never forget your promises to me your servant, for they are my only hope. They give me strength in all my troubles; how they refresh and revive me!

Psalm 119:49–50 TLB

BATHING BEAUTIES

One day I read the story of Jesus' baptism to my two boys. When I finished, I asked if they could tell me who baptized Jesus. The four year old, Shawn, jumped up and said, "I know, Mommy. I know. It was John the Bathtub."

Debbie Wilson, California

Come, follow me! And I will make you fishermen for the souls of men!

Mark 1:17 TLB

BIBLE MNEMONICS

One Sunday morning in children's church, I went around the room asking each child to name a book from the Old Testament. When I got to one little boy, he looked pensive and then said, "Sega." At first I thought he was trying to be the class clown. Then it dawned on me—Sega Genesis, the electronic video game!

Natalie Mangham, Ohio

The eyes of the Lord are on those who fear him, on those whose hope is in his unfailing love.

Psalm 33:18

FISHY FUNNY

My mother and I took my niece, age eight, to the zoo. While touring the Aqua Zoo, Amanda ran excitedly ahead. Above the next exhibit was a sign that read "Coins Kill Fish," so that the children would not throw pennies into the open water where fish were swimming. My niece read the sign and said to us, "Hey, come look at the coin-kill fish!"

Kristen Johnson, Pennsylvania

When you go through deep waters and great trouble, I will be with you. When you go through rivers of difficulty, you will not drown!

Isaiah 43:2 TLB

BANANA NANA

My sister has a precious goddaughter named KyMyra, whom she takes everywhere with her. KyMyra was waiting for her at the beauty salon when one of the other patrons introduced herself. KyMyra had difficulty pronouncing the woman's name, so the woman told her, "It's OK, honey, just call me 'Nana.'" KyMyra said, "I already have a nana, but I'll call you 'Ba'nana.'"

Kristal Rogers, Texas

Love is patient, love is kind. . . . it is not self-seeking, it is not easily angered, it keeps no record of wrongs. . . . It always protects, always trusts, always hopes, always perseveres.

1 Corinthians 13:4–7

HAPPY HELLO

My six-year-old son came home from Sunday school all excited because he had learned the Lord's Prayer. "Oh, good," I said, "let me hear you say it." He quickly recited, "Our Father, who art in heaven, hello! It be thy name."

Ruth Hultgren, Minnesota

You are members of God's very own family, citizens of God's country, and you belong in God's household with every other Christian.

Ephesians 2:19 TLB

HERE COMES THE BRIDE

For days after they'd been flower girls in a wedding, my two daughters played "wedding rehearsal" with a friend. One day they made guest lists; the next day they practiced marching down the hallway; then came the day to take the vows. My daughters stood arm-in-arm while their friend asked that all-important question, "Do you take this awful dreaded wife?"

Robin Kendle Parker, Texas

Those who trust in the Lord are like Mount Zion, which cannot be shaken but endures forever.

Psalm 125:1

THE OTHER ABE

One evening my five-year-old daughter and I read a Bible story together. When we finished, I quizzed her about it. "What was Abraham's name before God changed it?" I asked. She looked puzzled, then offered, "Lincoln?"

Annelle Maurer, California

A good name is more desirable than great riches; to be esteemed is better than silver or gold.

Proverbs 22:1

INTESTINAL INTEREST

As a prekindergarten teacher at a Christian school, I often teach Bible facts to the children. One day I told them that the Bible was made up of two sections containing sixty-six books in all. The next day I asked, "Who can tell me the names of the two sections of the Bible?" With great confidence, Tyler raised his hand and said, "The Old Intestine and the New Intestine."

Sharon Redd, Texas

Christ's righteousness makes men right with God, so that they can live.

Romans 5:18 TLB

MADE IN JAPAN

My grandfather was entertaining my five year old with action figures. Grandpa decided to probe Daniel's theological knowledge and asked if he knew God's last name. Daniel brightly responded, "I know! It's Zilla!"

Sara Marienthal, Missouri

I am the resurrection and the life. He who believes in me will live, even though he dies; and whoever lives and believes in me will never die.

John 11:25–26

ON HER OWN

My sister Kathy was in the process of buying a new car and was on the phone trying to get information about financing. Her five-year-old daughter, Hillary, wanted to know what she was talking about. "You wouldn't understand," Kathy told her. "I'm talking about a car loan. You don't even know what a loan is." "I do too know what a loan is," Hillary insisted. "It's when you're all by yourself."

Karen Aaker, California

He alone is my rock and my salvation; he is my fortress, I will never be shaken.

Psalm 62:2

THE COLA WARS

On our way home from church my husband asked three-year-old Charlotte, "What is your favorite song in Sunday school?" She replied, "Joshua fought the battle of Cherry Coke."

Ruth Skar, North Dakota

The Lord will defeat your enemies before you; they will march out together against you but scatter before you in seven directions!

Deuteronomy 28:7 TLB

KING OF THE CAR

While I was running errands one afternoon, my two boys began fighting over who was king of the car. Paul declared he was king, while David loudly protested he was king. Reminding them of their biblical namesakes, I explained that David was a king and Paul was an apostle. Paul grumbled as David gleefully exclaimed, "Yeah, I'm King David, and you're the impossible Paul!"

Maxine Stout, Michigan

No one who has become part of God's family makes a practice of sinning, for Christ, God's Son, holds him securely and the devil cannot get his hands on him.

1 John 5:18 TLB

KING OF THE JEWELS

One morning at the preschool where I teach, Sneha, a five-year-old Muslim girl, expressed curiosity about my crucifix pendant. "Who's that on your necklace?" "Jesus," I said. "He was a really rich man, wasn't he?" she queried. "Actually, not at all," I responded. "Jesus was a carpenter who led a very simple life." Puzzled, Sneha replied, "But wasn't He 'King of the Jewels'?"

Lee A. Schedler, Wisconsin

God is my salvation; I will trust and not be afraid. The Lord, the Lord, is my strength and my song; he has become my salvation.

Isaiah 12:2

SPIRITED REPLY

When my four-year-old son, Matthew, was dressing himself for preschool one morning, he chose to wear a pair of underpants with a Fruit of the Loom label inside. "Mommy," he explained to me, "I want to wear these because they have the fruit of the Spirit in them!"

Tammie Quesenberry, North Carolina

God gives special blessings to those who are humble.

1 Peter 5:5 TLB

VEGETARIAN SURPRISE

Our five-year-old daughter, Chara, was entertaining her five-year-old friend Isaac. When they let out our hunting dog to play, the dog immediately ran feverishly around the neighborhood and into the street. An oncoming car apparently had to come to an abrupt stop. As Chara and Isaac described the near miss to me, they were certain the poor pet's tail had been "runned over." Isaac exclaimed, "I just know it got hurt, and you'd better hurry and call a vegetarian!"

Melanie Miller, Kansas

Guide me in your truth and teach me, for you are God my Savior, and my hope is in you all day long.

Psalm 25:5

SPELLING STUMPER

Thrilled with her accomplishment of learning to spell, Jheri, my seven year old, was proudly spelling words for her grandpa one morning. Thinking he could stump her, he asked her to spell Mississippi. She very confidently stood up and said, "Mississippi—capital M-r-s period, capital S-i-p-y!"

Tina Hill, Wisconsin

No mere man has ever seen, heard or even imagined what wonderful things God has ready for those who love the Lord.

1 Corinthians 2:9 TLB

A PLANT FOR LIFE

My daughter's favorite song is "God Has a Plan for My Life." One day she announced, "God has a plan for my life too, Mommy." "He does?" I probed. "Yeah," she answered, "let me show you." Puzzled, I took her hand and followed her into her bedroom where she pointed to the shelf above her dresser. Right there, in all its green splendor, was God's plant for her life!

Samantha Sfirlea, Michigan

I will help you speak and will teach you what to say.

Exodus 4:12

KENTUCKY FRIED

My three-year-old son bounced out of Sunday school and announced they'd had "Chicken-in-a-Box" in class. The connection between the Bible and Kentucky Fried Chicken was a mystery to me until later that day when I heard that one of his classmates had come down with the childhood nemesis chicken pox!

Cheryl K. Ewings, Illinois

And the peace of God, which transcends all understanding, will guard your hearts and your minds in Christ Jesus.

Philippians 4:7

BAD COWBOYS

I was trying to explain my background to my three year old, Christa. I was describing gauchos—the Argentinean equivalent of cowboys—to her. "They dress in big shirts and pants and boots, carry a knife, and have long hair." With a concerned look, Christa looked up and asked, "Do they bite?"

Silvia L. Lakoduk, Idaho

He is good to everyone, and his compassion is intertwined with everything he does.

Psalm 145:9 TLB

CRAFTY SPELLER

While on vacation, my husband and I and our two sons stopped for breakfast at an oceanside restaurant. John, the four year old, was "reading" his place mat, which had puzzles, mazes, and a large pirate whose hat read "B.J. Squidley's." He was somewhat quiet as he spelled out, "B-J-S-Q-U-I-D-L-E-Y-S," and then, proud of himself, he blurted out, "That spells Mr. Pirateman!"

Kelly Steffen, Washington

Give generously, for your gifts will return to you later.

Ecclesiastes 11:1 TLB

WHAT KIND OF CHRISTIAN?

While I was driving my boys to swimming lessons, Michael, age eight, saw a book my husband had left in the car. He picked it up and read the title. "What's this book about?" he asked. "It's a book to help us become authentic Christians," I replied. He said, "Oh, yeah, that's what we are—right, Mom? Pathetic Christians."

Connie Schmotzer, Washington

He will call upon me, and I will answer him; I will be with him in trouble, I will deliver him and honor him.

Psalm 91:15

NAME NIBBLINGS

My boss's five-year-old daughter came to visit us at work and tell the staff about her newborn baby sister. She said, "Her first name is Brittany, her middle name is Marie, but we haven't decided on a last name yet!"

Joyce Flakes, Texas

I will bind you to me forever with chains of righteousness and justice and love and mercy.

Hosea 2:19 TLB

THE SCARIEST DISCIPLE

Last summer I taught a vacation Bible school class on Judas's betrayal of Jesus. After the lesson, I went over the review questions and asked, "Who betrayed Jesus for thirty pieces of silver?" Without hesitating, my seven-year-old son, Kenny, replied, "I know! It was Judas the Scariest!"

Karen Weaver, Ohio

As far as the east is from the west, so far has he removed our transgressions from us.

Psalm 103:12

LOADED QUESTION

After church one Sunday, my friend Betsey's young son asked, "Mom, what's a virgin?" *Oh, no,* she thought. *The time has come.* So Betsey sat down with him and calmly explained the facts of life in great detail. When she finished, he exclaimed, "No, Mom, not that kind of virgin. I was talking about the King James Virgin."

Kristy Roberts Dykes, Florida

Since the Truth is in our hearts forever, God the Father and Jesus Christ his Son will bless us with great mercy and much peace, and with truth and love.

2 John 1:2–3 TLB

GOOD NEWS FOR PRESBYTERIANS

I listened casually as my nine year old recited the bicycle safety rules he had to memorize for a scouting merit badge. "Obey all traffic rules. Drive with traffic, not against it. Use hand signals for turning or stopping," he recited. He caught my full attention, however, when he said, "All Presbyterians have the right of way."

Susan Simmons, Tennessee

Let us come boldly to the very throne of God and stay there to receive his mercy and to find grace to help us in our times of need.

Hebrews 4:16 TLB

HOUNDS OF HEAVEN

When our two year old used the word "salvation" in a conversation one day, I thought I should ask if she understood what the word meant. "I know all about it, Mommy," she said. "We saw it at the movies." I was puzzled. The only movie she had ever seen was a Disney production. "What movie?" I asked. "You know," she replied, somewhat impatiently, "101 Salvations!"

Marcia Ford, Delaware

In his great mercy he has given us new birth into a living hope through the resurrection of Jesus Christ from the dead, and into an inheritance that can never perish, spoil or fade—kept in heaven for you.

1 Peter 1:3–4

WHAT HE SAID

While attending an aunt's funeral, my four year old, David, sat between his Uncle John and me. After reading John 3:16, the pastor noted that it could be found in the gospel according to John. Those around us smiled as David looked at his uncle and asked, "Uncle John, did you really say that?"

M. Doris Murphy, Maine

Blessed are those whose strength is in you, who have set their hearts on pilgrimage. . . . They go from strength to strength, till each appears before God in Zion.

Psalm 84:5, 7

Food Fun

PRACTICAL HELPER

One Saturday, Jessica, my four-year-old godchild, was "helping" her parents paint a mural of Christ on the wall of her Sunday school room. After a while Jessica got hungry and asked, "Will you open my crackers?" Her mother answered that she'd have to wait until they could wash the paint off their hands. With a mix of impatience and absolute faith, Jessica approached the mural and asked, "Jesus, will You open my crackers?"

Kate Vander Sluis, California

For he has not despised my cries of deep despair; he has not turned and walked away. When I cried to him, he heard and came.

Psalm 22:24 TLB

COMMUNION CONFUSION

When my daughter, Laura, was three, she went with me to buy some grape juice for our church's Communion service. Telling her it was for the Lord's Supper, I put it in the refrigerator. Later, her brother, six-year-old Jonathan, saw it and wanted some. "No," Laura scolded. "That's for God's lunch!"

Melanie Bell, Texas

For God did not send his Son into the world to condemn the world, but to save the world through him.

John 3:17

COLORFUL THINKER

One evening my daughter, Leah, watched while I gathered the ingredients for spaghetti sauce. As I grabbed the green pepper, Leah asked, "Mommy, what's that?" I told her it was a green pepper. "Oh," Leah replied, "where's the green salt?"

Richa Clark, North Carolina

You have become living building-stones for God's use in building his house. What's more, you are his holy priests; so come to him.

1 Peter 2:5 TLB

SEED OF A DIFFERENT KIND

My four year old, Kelsey, and I were on our way to Grandma's house when she found a sesame seed on the seat next to her. "Mommy, can I plant this when we get to Grandma's house?" "Sure," I said. "What are you going to grow with it?" She looked at me as if this were the most ridiculous question I'd ever asked her and replied, "Cheeseburgers!"

Lisa Skaggs, Ohio

The Lord will indeed give what is good.

Psalm 85:12

JACK SPRAT COULD EAT NO FAT

When our family had to make some drastic changes in our eating habits due to my husband's high cholesterol, dinner conversation often turned to the grams of fat in the food. One evening our four year old, Amanda, looked at me curiously and asked, "Mom, which grandma is Grandma Fat?"

Kari Christensen, Florida

I the Lord do not change.

Malachi 3:6

HOUND CAKE

I made a German chocolate cake to celebrate my father-in-law's birthday. The next day my six-year-old son, Ryan, asked, "Hey, Mom, do we have any more of that German shepherd cake?"

Mary Belville, Michigan

Therefore he is able to save completely those who come to God through him, because he always lives to intercede for them.

Hebrews 7:25

FROSTING FETISH

One Sunday my husband, our two boys, and I were having breakfast with my parents before church. My son Jon, quite the sweets lover, was ecstatic when my mom said we were having frosted cinnamon rolls and milk. He waited somewhat impatiently and finally received his plate. After a moment of silence, he looked up and declared, "Hey, who put bread on my frosting?"

Kathy Gnidovic, Illinois

If you belong to the Lord, reverence him; for everyone who does this has everything he needs.

Psalm 34:9 TLB

CHOCOLATE CHORTLES

One night my teenage daughter, Deborah, had a lot of homework. After dinner, I tried to encourage her by saying, "Well, honey, when you get it done, I'll have some fresh-baked chocolate chip cookies ready for you." "Oh, Mom!" she responded in teenage despair, "even chocolate can't help a woman now!"

Linda Garrison, Oregon

May the God of hope fill you with all joy and peace as you trust in him, so that you may overflow with hope by the power of the Holy Spirit.

Romans 15:13

WET THEOLOGY

After taking a big gulp of milk one day, my three-year-old daughter said, "Mommy, Jesus is getting wet." "He is?" I asked. "Why do you say that?" "Because I'm taking a drink, and Jesus lives in here," she responded, smiling and pointing to her heart.

Lynette Kittle, California

For no matter how many promises God has made, they are "Yes" in Christ.

2 Corinthians 1:20

PATTY CAKE

When my daughter, Grace, said she didn't need a cake for her seventh birthday party, I told her that the guests usually expected cake and that it was our way of saying "Thank you for coming." Some time later, when the time arrived to serve cake at the party, Grace piped up, "Now, here's your pay for coming!"

Susan Lachner, California

The Lord our God is merciful.

Daniel 9:9

HAM AND CHEESE ON RYE

During our church's story time for young children, the storyteller was quizzing the group on the account of Jesus feeding the five thousand. After she showed a basket, she asked, "What was in this?" "Fish and bread," came the reply. Then looking to my daughter, who was three and a half at the time, she asked, "Chelsea, do you know what they did with the bread?" Chelsea pursed her lips in thought, then boldly proclaimed, "Made ham and cheese sandwiches!"

Lynette Fasnacht, Pennsylvania

Every word of God is flawless; he is a shield to those who take refuge in him.

Proverbs 30:5

CLEVER EATER

Our son, Daniel, was eating his dinner. He ate his hamburger, then his baked beans, but neglected his broccoli. When I told him his broccoli was calling him, he responded, "No, it's not. I can't hear it!" "Yes, it is," I insisted. He responded, "But my beans were calling me first—and now I'm full!"

Bobbie Zimmerman, Minnesota

Let us not get tired of doing what is right, for after a while we will reap a harvest of blessing if we don't get discouraged and give up.

Galatians 6:9 TLB

PARTICULAR ABOUT POTATOES

I was busy preparing dinner for a sick neighbor when my two-year-old son, Jacob, asked me what I was making. I said I was making au gratin potatoes. Jacob looked puzzled and said, "Mama, they won't eat all rotten potatoes!"

Margaret Flannery, Michigan

He gives food to every living thing, for his lovingkindness continues forever.

Psalm 136:25 TLB

DIET DOLDRUMS

When we moved to England, we discovered that refrigerators there are smaller than we are used to in the United States. So when we invited friends over for a barbecue, it filled quickly with salads and desserts. One unusually hot day, I taped the refrigerator door shut, hoping the food would remain cold until supper. Accustomed to the variety of diets we try, my youngest son, hungry after a morning of helping his dad and older brother in the yard, asked disappointedly, "Mom, the fridge door is taped shut. Are we on a diet again?"

Michelle A. Pablo, Great Britain

Keep yourselves in God's love as you wait for the mercy of our Lord Jesus Christ to bring you to eternal life.

Jude 1:21

EAST OF EDEN

One day my son Jonathan came home from preschool with a picture of Adam and Eve he had colored. He began to tell me the story of creation, and it seemed he had his facts down pretty well. "Adam and Eve disobeyed God because they ate the fruit God told them not to eat," he explained. Impressed by how much he knew, I pointed to the picture and asked, "What's this place called?" Jonathan replied earnestly, "The Garden of Eating."

Laura Groves, Florida

I have created you and cared for you since you were born.

Isaiah 46:3 TLB

WILD THING

While I was preparing to mix up a batch of our favorite cookies, three-year-old Jacob wandered into the kitchen and asked if he could help. "Sure!" I replied. "What would you like to do?" He matter-of-factly replied, "I want to beat the eggs with the wild wisk!"

Audrey Thomas, Minnesota

I am the Lord, the God of all mankind; is there anything too hard for me?

Jeremiah 32:27 TLB

FULL MOON

My grandmother told me about a conversation that took place when I was three. Standing outside her house one night, I called excitedly, "Grandmama, come see the moon!" As she rushed out, she asked, "Why? Is it full?" I responded, "No, it hasn't eaten yet."

Angie Curry, Kansas

The Lord is near to all who call on him, to all who call on him in truth.

Psalm 145:18

HUMPTY DUMPTY

I was at the kitchen counter making dinner. As usual, my two-year-old daughter was standing on a chair next to me, playing in the sink. I picked up an egg and cracked it open on the edge of my mixing bowl. She looked at me and soothingly said, "Don't worry, Mommy. Daddy will fix the egg. He fixes everything."

Carole Anderson, Michigan

Every spiritual gift and power for doing his will are yours.

1 Corinthians 1:7 TLB

EYES ON THE PIES

During a recent pie social at our church, the pastor was presented with a birthday gift. The acceptance speech he gave was quite lengthy, and our four year old grew impatient. Seeing all those pies, and not being able to eat, required patience he didn't have. Suddenly, rather loudly, he stated, "Hey! I thought that this was supposed to be a party!"

Cynthia Cox, Arizona

Your strong love for each other will prove to the world that you are my disciples.

John 13:35 TLB

OUT OF WHACK

We were having trouble getting our youngest son, Sean, to eat his meals. One night at dinner I told him that, if he didn't start eating better, his stomach would get out of whack and we'd have to take him to the hospital. As we bowed our heads, Sean prayed, "Dear God, thank You for this food and help me eat it so I don't have to go to the hospital and get some more whack. Amen."

Gail Breach, Pennsylvania

Though I am surrounded by troubles, you will bring me safely through them.

Psalm 138:7 TLB

MILK QUANDARY

While I was pregnant with our daughter, Hannah, my inquisitive five-year-old son, Jonathan, and I discussed why I drank skim milk and he drank 2 percent. Shortly after I gave birth, we were sitting together on the couch while I nursed Hannah. He watched for a while and then inquired, "Mom, is that skim milk or 2 percent?"

Brenda Wood, Ohio

God has said, "Never will I leave you; never will I forsake you."
Hebrews 13:5

BLESSED HOPE

My three year old, Evan, and I were eating breakfast when he asked, "What if there were no God, Mommy?" I replied, "Oh, the world would be a very sad place. There would be no salvation, no love, and no hope." He looked very serious and responded, "Yeah, and there would be no blessing, and we couldn't eat our food!"

Terry Lynn Manning, Georgia

This certain hope of being saved is a strong and trustworthy anchor for our souls, connecting us with God himself.
Hebrews 6:19 TLB

CINNAMON TWIST

My mother always put cinnamon in our applesauce for added flavor when we were kids. Of course, this changed not only the flavor but the color as well. One day my nephew, Jeff, was visiting and got to try some of Grandma's cinnamon applesauce. He tasted it and commented, "Grandma, we have this at our house, too, only ours isn't dirty!"

Jill Burrell, Michigan

He fulfills the desires of those who reverence and trust him.

Psalm 145:19 TLB

A GOOD WORKOUT

I was getting some tomatoes out of the refrigerator and picked up one that was mushy. When I told my four-year-old son, "Boy, this one's not in very good shape," he replied with a chuckle, "I guess it didn't get a good workout, Mom."

Dianne B. Martin, Tennessee

Whoever humbles himself like this child is the greatest in the kingdom of heaven.

Matthew 18:4

CHURCH CHUCKLES

PLAYING CHURCH

When my daughter was three, she asked me to play church with her. What could she have in mind? I wondered. She took me by the hand, led me to her play chairs all lined up like pews, waved her arms, and commanded, "Now sit down." I did. "Now stand up." I did. "Now sit down . . . now stand up . . ."

Roberta C. Fish, New Jersey

Surely I am with you always, to the very end of the age.

Matthew 28:20

WET WISH

One Sunday while my husband was preaching, a visiting minister held our two-year-old daughter, Christie. As her dad reached the altar call portion of his message, the visiting minister whispered to her, "Would you like Jesus to change you?" Her earnest reply was, "Yeah, I'm wet."

Donna Sapienza, Massachusetts

I waited patiently for the Lord; he turned to me and heard my cry.

Psalm 40:1

LAST MEAL

Our pastor had preached a sermon on the Last Supper. As we drove home, our son, David, was quiet and seemed sad. When I asked him what was wrong, he said, "It must be awful to be poor." Wondering what brought these thoughts on, I queried, "Why are you thinking about that, honey?" "Because," he stated emphatically, "the pastor said it was those guys' last supper!"

Kay Ammon, Alabama

With long life will I satisfy him and show him my salvation.

Psalm 91:16

JUST DO IT

I've often wondered how much my children really pay attention at church—and how much they really understand. One Sunday my three-year-old daughter listened as the minister expounded loudly on how Christians ought to be helping their fellow man. I was intently listening when the minister almost shouted, "And just what are we doing about it?" To my surprise, my daughter enthusiastically shouted, "NOTHING!" I will never again underestimate my children's listening capabilities.

Martha N. Wolowicz, Minnesota

Christ has given each of us special abilities—whatever he wants us to have out of his rich storehouse of gifts.

Ephesians 4:7 TLB

COLOR BIND

Our three-year-old daughter, Lindsay, is used to attending Sunday school in a separate classroom where the children listen to Bible stories, sing songs, and color pictures. After a special family service during which she joined the rest of the family in the sanctuary, we asked what she thought of the grown-ups' church. She looked around the room, then thoughtfully replied, "It's very nice—but where do you keep your crayons?"

Sam Todd, California

You have made known to me the path of life; you will fill me with joy in your presence, with eternal pleasures at your right hand.

Psalm 16:11

PLAY BALL!

Since his older brothers are very athletic, my four-year-old son, Curtis, has attended sporting events since he was an infant. One Sunday morning in church, Curtis was becoming increasingly restless. Finally he grabbed my arm and asked, "Mom, is it halftime yet?"

Taffy Pfaehler, Indiana

If you will humble yourselves under the mighty hand of God, in his good time he will lift you up.

1 Peter 5:6 TLB

PENNIES FOR HIS THOUGHTS

My grade-school-age daughter, Emily, fidgeted nonstop during our new pastor's first sermon. After twenty minutes of sighing and wiggling, she turned to me and whispered, "Mom, does this guy get paid to do this?" I smiled and nodded my head. Ten more minutes passed, and his sermon still wasn't close to conclusion. Again Emily tugged at my arm and in a low voice said, "How much?"

Nancy Stoffregen Depa, Illinois

The Lord is compassionate and gracious, slow to anger, abounding in love.

Psalm 103:8

KID GENIUS

In a morning church service, our Daniel watched in awe as an eight-year-old boy that he knew played an instrumental solo. Afterward, Daniel was uncharacteristically quiet on the way home. Then he said, "Wow! That was great! Does he drive a car too?"

Kathy Gardaphé, Illinois

If we are faithful to the end, trusting God just as we did when we first became Christians, we will share in all that belongs to Christ.

Hebrews 3:14 TLB

NEWSFLASH!

My five-year-old grandson, Derek, was sitting with me during our morning worship service. The special music that Sunday was by a couple who sang "I've Just Seen Jesus." Although he was busily playing with some toys, I knew he was listening when he looked up at me and said, "Grandma, where did they see Him?"

Rosie Tucker, Indiana

For he chose us in him before the creation of the world to be holy and blameless in his sight.

Ephesians 1:4

CLOWNING AROUND

One Sunday morning in our small rural church, my husband stood to offer his pastoral prayer. I bowed my head as my two daughters quietly thumbed through pew Bibles. Suddenly the five year old nudged me and exclaimed in an excited whisper, "Look, Mommy, I can read the Bible! It says right here, 'Ruth meets Bozo'!"

Karen Wingate, Kansas

Those who love your laws have great peace of heart and mind and do not stumble.

Psalm 119:165 TLB

ME TOO!

When our two year old, Heidi, sat in "big people's church" for the first time, she watched the Communion plate pass from person to person. Then she watched the tray of little cups go by right under her nose. Heidi leaned forward, puzzled, her eyes following the tray as it traveled the row and on to the people behind us. As it got farther and farther away, she grew incredulous. She scrambled to her feet, hands on hips, sternly looked at me, and stage-whispered, "Hey! I didn't get no 'freshments!"

Frances Pullen, California

God has already given you everything you need. . . . He has given you all of the present and all of the future. All are yours.

1 Corinthians 3:21–22 TLB

QUIRKY QUARTET

One Sunday night a quartet from a nearby college came to sing for our church. As the four young men in matching gray trousers and navy blazers began to sing, one little girl turned to her mother, pointed, and exclaimed, "Hey, look! They all have different heads!"

Melba Ferrell, Tennessee

God is good, and he loves goodness; the godly shall see his face.

Psalm 11:7 TLB

GOD IN THE PEW

Four-year-old Jonathon had become a good listener at Sunday school and church, but he was still confused by some things. For instance, on Youth Sunday the pastor did not wear his usual robes; instead he sat with the congregation just down the pew from Jonathan and his mom, Suzanne. In the middle of the service, Jonathon loudly whispered in awed tones, "Mom, God is sitting next to me." "No, Jonathon, that's not God," answered Suzanne, who wanted to straighten out his theology. "Then is it Jesus?" he queried.

Kathleen Hicks, Tennessee

Fear not, for I am with you. Do not be dismayed. I am your God. I will strengthen you; I will help you; I will uphold you with my victorious right hand.

Isaiah 41:10 TLB

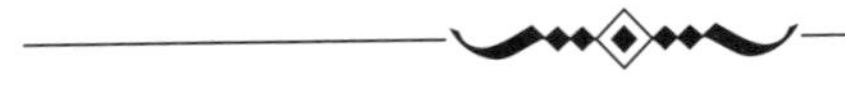

DOING TIME

One day as I was working in the church nursery, I overheard a three-year-old girl talking to her mom. "Mommy," she asked, "when Jesus takes us to heaven, will I have to go to the nursery?"

Chandra Drury, California

Those who teach God's laws and obey them shall be great in the Kingdom of Heaven.

Matthew 5:19 TLB

FREE ADMITTANCE

One day when my daughter was four, we were running late for Sunday school, and they had already taken up the offering when she got to her class. After church, she came skipping out to the parking lot, holding her offering in her hand. "Mommy!" she exclaimed. "I got in free today."

Betty Grigsby, Alabama

[He] satisfies your desires with good things so that your youth is renewed like the eagle's.

Psalm 103:5

PRESTO, CHANGE-O

While my three younger sisters and I were growing up, our parents would tell us every Sunday morning that we were going to God's house to worship. One Sunday, we had a visiting minister. Out of the blue and loud enough for all to hear, my youngest sister said, "Hey, did we get a new God?"

Tracey Kruckenberg, Nebraska

Since he himself has now been through suffering and temptation, he knows what it is like when we suffer and are tempted, and he is wonderfully able to help us.

Hebrews 2:18 TLB

DRENCHED IN THE SPIRIT

My seven-year-old son was baptized at nearby Lake Tahoe. With tears streaming down my face, I watched as he came out of the water, then excitedly asked if he felt different. "Yeah, Mom, I do," he replied. "Now I have water up my nose!"

Leslie A. Williamson, Nevada

Ask and you will receive, and your joy will be complete.

John 16:24

HARD SELL

When we invited a neighbor boy to go to church with us, he was very hard to impress. As the pastor spoke of God's care for us—so all-encompassing that He even knows the number of hairs on our heads—the boy just stared at our nearly bald pastor and shook his head. "Well, that's not so hard," he said.

Janet Riehecky, Illinois

I have set the Lord always before me. Because he is at my right hand, I will not be shaken.

Psalm 16:8

TALK, TALK, TALK

My three-year-old daughter, Laryssa, usually finds it hard to sit through a church service. One Sunday morning was particularly hard because we'd been at the church for a long time. During the sermon, she sat still for a few minutes, looking at the pastor, until finally blurting out, "Mom, is he talking to himself?"

Ann Marquardt, Wisconsin

After you have suffered a little while, our God, who is full of kindness through Christ, will give you his eternal glory. He personally will come and pick you up, and set you firmly in place, and make you stronger than ever.

1 Peter 5:10 TLB

CONFUSED FEET

When our son was four years old, he proudly dressed himself for church one Sunday. In our haste, I didn't realize that his shoes were on the wrong feet. As we went through the receiving line after the service, the pastor whispered to him that his shoes were on the wrong feet. Glancing first down at his feet and then up at the pastor, our puzzled son said, "But, pastor, these are the only feet I have."

Wilette Wehner, New Mexico

He will not let your foot slip—he who watches over you will not slumber.

Psalm 121:3

JUST CALL HER MONEYBAGS

Our church sponsors a "pennies for missions" project where members deposit coins in cans placed throughout the church. I'm responsible for counting, wrapping, and depositing the coins in the bank. One month, the amount collected was more than I could carry alone, so I asked my busy teenage son for a hand. The afternoon we planned to make the deposit, his band director announced a last-minute practice. My son promptly raised his hand and to a surprised group announced, "I won't be able to stay for practice today. I have to help my mom carry her money to the bank."

Judith L. Cerra, Pennsylvania

The Lord God is coming with mighty power; he will rule with awesome strength. See, his reward is with him, to each as he has done.

Isaiah 40:10 TLB

A BIG SURPRISE

My two granddaughters, aged five and six, were in church with me. The pastor was closing his sermon, so he asked everyone to close their eyes. I overheard the six year old tell her sister, Brianna, "He said to close our eyes. We have to do it so we'll get a big surprise."

Patricia Puckett, California

Speak to one another with psalms, hymns and spiritual songs. Sing and make music in your heart to the Lord, always giving thanks to God.

Ephesians 5:19–20

WALKING SERMON

As our pastor's sermon stretched on, my daughter grew impatient and started to talk. "Shh," I whispered. "I want to hear the sermon." Later that week, we saw the pastor while shopping. We exchanged greetings, and as we walked away, I asked my daughter, "Do you know who that was?" "Sure," she replied. "That was the Sermon."

Helen Siml, Illinois

For where two or three gather together because they are mine, I will be right there among them.

Matthew 18:20 TLB

ANYBODY HOME?

Every month before attending my Bible study at church, I would tell my three year old, Chad, that we were going to God's house. Each time we walked through the quiet sanctuary on our way to the nursery, Chad looked around in awe. One particular day, he stopped abruptly and asked, "Mommy, if this is God's house, how come He's never home?"

Karen Ketzler, Indiana

On this rock I will build my church, and the gates of Hades will not overcome it.

Matthew 16:18

HOMEMADE HUMOR

TAKE ME OUT TO THE BALL GAME

Our two year old eagerly attended his father's weekly softball games and was disappointed whenever a game was played too late in the evening for him to attend. I hadn't realized how bad he felt about missing these games until I noticed a subtle revision in a story he recently told me. He said, "Cinderella was sad because he couldn't go to the ball game."

Karen E. Hilverda, Michigan

In the day of my trouble I will call to you, for you will answer me.

Psalm 86:7

LITTLE ACCOUNTANT

One day a little boy came to the register at the bookstore where I work. He paid for his book with a five dollar bill. I counted his change and asked, "Would you like a bag?" His reply was serious and honest. "No, but I would like some more change."

Anne Marie Bennett, Massachusetts

Trust in the Lord God always, for in the Lord Jehovah is your everlasting strength.

Isaiah 26:4 TLB

TIME TALES

My ten-year-old daughter and I had been busy cleaning our backyard when I asked her to go see what time it was. She came back a few minutes later and replied, "It's a quarter to seven thirty."

Shirley Redmond, Arizona

We were chosen from the beginning to be his, and all things happen just as he decided long ago.

Ephesians 1:11 TLB

THE GREAT ESCAPE

Ever since my four-year-old nephew, Matthew, has been old enough to understand, his mom has told him Jesus is in his heart. One day, after playing in the yard for hours, he ran up to his mother out of breath. Holding his hand over his furiously beating heart, he exclaimed, "Mommy, I think Jesus is trying to get out!"

Rhonda Meadows, Virginia

Day by day the Lord also pours out his steadfast love upon me.

Psalm 42:8 TLB

MR. DONUTHEAD

My friend was taking her young son to the barber shop after a routine visit to his doctor, a kindly older gentleman with only a small ring of hair around the sides of his head. Just before entering the barber shop, the boy said, "Mom, can I get a donut haircut?" Confused, my friend asked, "What is that?" Matter-of-factly her son replied, "You know, Mom. It's like my doctor has."

Teresia Gravley Thomason, Georgia

All those who know your mercy, Lord, will count on you for help. For you have never yet forsaken those who trust in you.

Psalm 9:10 TLB

NO BONES ABOUT IT

When my daughter, Marisa, was two and a half, we were eating popcorn. As she got closer to the bottom of the bag, she peered in, grabbed an unpopped kernel, and said, "Mom, did you know this popcorn has bones?"

Rhonda Mendoza, Texas

Only the Lord knows! He searches all hearts and examines deepest motives so he can give to each person his right reward, according to his deeds—how he has lived.

Jeremiah 17:10 TLB

PANTY DEFECT

For several difficult weeks I tried to potty-train our two-and-a-half-year-old son, Joseph. One day, after I had changed his third set of dirty panties, he looked up at me and said, "Mom, we need to take these panties back—they just don't work!"

Christine Bushman, Illinois

Each one of you has put to flight a thousand of the enemy, for the Lord your God fights for you, just as he has promised.

Joshua 23:10 TLB

BETTER CHECK . . .

After explaining to my four-year-old son why he couldn't watch the Power Ranger TV show, I told him that when he was a daddy, he could watch whatever he wanted. "I'm going to let my little boy watch the Power Rangers," he replied. "After I check with my wife first."

Suzy Ryan, California

I will pour out my Spirit on all people.

Joel 2:28

BOY AND GIRL BUGS

One day when our son, Daniel, was over at his grandmother Mimi's house, they were discussing the ceramic ladybug magnets on the refrigerator. Mimi was telling Daniel many facts about ladybugs when Daniel interrupted her and asked, "Mimi, do ladybugs live with boybugs?"

Daniella Johnson, North Dakota

I will praise the Lord, who counsels me; even at night my heart instructs me.

Psalm 16:7

THE HOLE TRUTH

While visiting my grandparents on their Iowa farm, my three-year-old daughter, Sarah, was intrigued by all the sheep, the horses, the cows, and the red barn. But as a city-bred kid used to indoor plumbing, what fascinated her the most was the "two-holer" outhouse. Upon her first visit there, she opened the door, looked back at my grandmother, and asked, "How come you've got two holes, and we've only got one?"

Arlene Sampson, Iowa

The eternal God is your Refuge, and underneath are the everlasting arms.

Deuteronomy 33:27 TLB

CALL IT!

My husband and our five-year-old son, Steven, were having fun flipping a quarter and calling "heads or tails" to make decisions. A short while later, Steven ran in with a nickel he'd found outside and said, "Dad, flip this one—heads or hotels!"

Kay Murphree, Tennessee

Come to me, all you who are weary and burdened, and I will give you rest.

Matthew 11:28

RUNAWAY EMOTIONS

As I was having my devotions one morning, I heard my three-year-old daughter, Kayla, answer the telephone in the next room. Trying not to burst out laughing, I listened as she told the caller, "My mom is having her emotions now. Can she call you back?"

Kelly Kennard, Ohio

"Because he loves me," says the Lord, "I will rescue him; I will protect him, for he acknowledges my name."

Psalm 91:14

HOOKED

When my family was fishing near our lake cabin one day, we taught our five-year-old daughter, Emily, how to bait a fishhook. A passing neighbor, observing her squirming line, inquired, "Did you put those worms on yourself, little girl?" Emily looked at him incredulously and replied, "No, I put them on my hook!"

Loretta Elder Brown, North Carolina

I have loved you, O my people, with an everlasting love; with lovingkindness I have drawn you to me.

Jeremiah 31:3 TLB

BIRTHDAY INVITATION

Our five year old was looking at a wall calendar containing a picture of a log cabin on a certain day. "What's happening that day?" he asked. "That's Abraham Lincoln's birthday," I replied. With grinning anticipation, he asked, "Are we invited?"

Marion L. Jones, Virginia

You love righteousness and hate wickedness; therefore God, your God, has set you above your companions by anointing you with the oil of joy.

Psalm 45:7

SHOWER SURPRISE

Before I left home to attend a baby shower, I explained to our four year old, Frannie, and her three-year-old sister, Allie, that I was going to a shower with ladies from the church. While I was gone, my husband put the girls in bed. When I got home and went to their room to say good night, Allie asked, "Did you have a good time, Mommy?" I said I did, and she hugged me. Then she looked up and asked, "But, Mommy, how come you're not wet? I thought you were going to take a shower with those ladies!"

Kendra Halbert, Alaska

If anyone obeys his word, God's love is truly made complete in him. This is how we know we are in him: Whoever claims to live in him must walk as Jesus did.

1 John 2:5–6

PESKY PACKAGE

I was waiting for my plane in the airport terminal when a family walked up to the check-in counter with a very upset little boy. After several long minutes of nonstop crying, a young boy standing in line behind them turned to his mother and said, "Can't they put him with the luggage?"

Susan Knopf, Washington

God is our refuge and strength, an ever-present help in trouble.

Psalm 46:1

JUST ADD WATER

One evening while my daughters were taking a bath together, four-year-old Andrea began pouring water over her ten-month-old sister's bald little head. Exasperated, I asked Andrea what she was doing. Without a moment's hesitation, she replied, "I'm watering Rachel's head so her hair will grow!"

Shelley Toren, Michigan

Be really glad—because these trials will make you partners with Christ in his suffering, and afterwards you will have the wonderful joy of sharing his glory in that coming day when it will be displayed.

1 Peter 4:13 TLB

RURAL SHOPPING

My daughter, Laura, and I often escape rural life and go shopping in the city. The frequency of these trips became apparent recently when we visited my grandparents' farm. Laura pointed to the cows and asked, "Are those for sale?" "No, honey, why?" I replied. "Well," she paused with a perplexed look on her face, "they all have price tags on their ears!"

Marilyn Stroup, Kansas

We are in God because we are in Jesus Christ his Son, who is the only true God; and he is eternal Life.

1 John 5:20 TLB

WHISKER PHILOSOPHY

One evening, my son, Benjamin, was drawing a picture of a rabbit. He'd drawn the head—complete with ears, eyes, and a nose. "What else does it need, Mom?" he asked. I suggested whiskers. "Mom," he replied, "I'm not making a daddy bunny."

Darlene Stiefel, New Jersey

From the fullness of his grace we have all received one blessing after another. For the law was given through Moses; grace and truth came through Jesus Christ.

John 1:16–17

BEAR WITH ME

When my daughter was three, she received a hand-me-down brown fake-fur coat. She tried it on and, while thoughtfully examining the "fur covered" buttons, commented, "I didn't know bears grew buttons!"

Carol Johnson, California

When he comes back he will take these dying bodies of ours and change them into glorious bodies like his own, using the same mighty power that he will use to conquer all else everywhere.

Philippians 3:21 TLB

FROSTY EFFECTS

Maire, a perky three-year-old student, was taking off her snow scarf one bitter January morning. "Mommy," she began, "when it gets this cold, my cheeks get red, and then my eyes start to drool."

Ann Skodje Redding, Minnesota

What a God he is! How perfect in every way! All his promises prove true.

Psalm 18:30 TLB

AT THE END OF HER ROPE

My four year old desperately wanted a jump rope so she could "jump like the big girls" she'd seen on *Sesame Street.* When I brought one home for her she was overjoyed. But try as she might, she just couldn't get the hang of it. When her frustration peaked, she handed me the rope and said, "You'll just have to take this one back, Mommy. It doesn't work."

Cathy Blake, Colorado

The Lord your God is the faithful God who for a thousand generations keeps his promises and constantly loves those who love him and who obey his commands.

Deuteronomy 7:9 TLB

MOONSTRUCK

"Look, Mom, the moon's still up!" my young son exclaimed while looking out the window one morning. "Why is it so high?" he inquired. "God put it up there for many reasons," I said and rattled off a few. Still trying to figure it out, he looked up at me and asked, "Did God put it that high so little kids can't touch it?"

Lynne Allen, New Jersey

You are God, my only place of refuge.

Psalm 43:2 TLB

RAINY FACE

During a trip to visit my grandparents, we watched a television documentary about a man with AIDS who was finally reunited with his parents. As I began to cry while watching it, my two-year-old daughter walked up and asked, "Mom, why is it raining on your face?"

Kimberly LeBlanc, Texas

The Lord is full of compassion and mercy.

James 5:11

UDDERLY CONFUSED

When our family arrived at the county fair, our three-year-old daughter wanted to visit the animals first. As we walked down a row of prize-winning dairy cows, Melissa excitedly pointed and said, "Look, I see their gutters!"

Kelly A. Kim, California

He rescues the poor who are godly and gives them many children and much prosperity.

Psalm 107:41 TLB

CLEANING CREW

At one particularly overwhelming moment, just after I'd walked past several piles of dirty laundry to get to my kitchen where the dishes were piled high, I threw up my hands in exasperation and exclaimed, "My life's a mess!" No sooner had the words left my lips than I heard my three-year-old son, Jacob, chirp, "Then sweep it up!"

Jane Schmidt, Oregon

Do not be afraid, for I am with you.

Isaiah 43:5

STRIP CONNECTIONS

At the supermarket one day, I noticed a woman in her fifties, dressed in a business suit. She had finally worked her way through the slowest line to the checkout stand. Suddenly, above the din of disgruntled customers, a small child said excitedly, "Look, Mama, there's the striptease lady from our church!" The woman turned, smiled, and said in a voice that matched the volume of the child's, "You mean the film strip lady!"

Elizabeth Eichenberger, California

I will bless those who bless you and curse those who curse you; and the entire world will be blessed because of you.

Genesis 12:3 TLB

A STEP IN THE RIGHT DIRECTION?

One morning my three-year-old son, Joel, practiced dressing himself. After a long struggle to get his socks on, he finally plopped down on the floor in front of me with a shoe in each hand. "Now let's see," he said, looking at each shoe in turn. "This one goes on my right foot—and this one goes on my wrong foot!"

Nancy Martin, Virgin Islands

God will shed his own glorious light upon you. He will heal you; your godliness will lead you forward, and goodness will be a shield before you, and the glory of the Lord will protect you from behind.

Isaiah 58:8 TLB

THE EXTRA MILE

Jed, my three year old, accidentally bumped into me and apologized by saying, "Sorry, is that enough?" Later in the day he bumped me again and apologized with, "Sorry, is that enough?" I was getting curious, so I asked, "What if it isn't enough?" Sweetly he replied, "Oh, then I would kiss you."

Vicki Davis, Texas

Blessed are the merciful, for they will be shown mercy.

Matthew 5:7

. . . AND IT SHALL BE OPENED

When we purchased our minivan, our family gathered in the parking lot to thank God. My husband prayed, "Thank you, Jesus, for opening the door for us to get this van . . ." After considerable thought, Daniel, the three year old, said, "Daddy, Jesus doesn't need to open the door for us—you just use the key!"

Gina Vaughn, Georgia

The Lord will stay with you as long as you stay with him! Whenever you look for him, you will find him.

2 Chronicles 15:2 TLB

TOUGH THURSDAYS

My husband and I told our son, Adam, not to go inside our neighbor's house without our permission. One day he went in to play. While we were scolding him, we asked why he disobeyed. He began to cry and asked, "What day of the week is it?" Puzzled by the question, his dad offered, "Thursday. Why?" Adam brightened a little. "I don't have a very good memory on Thursdays."

Sherry Holsted, Tennessee

Let love and faithfulness never leave you; bind them around your neck, write them on the tablet of your heart. Then you will win favor and a good name in the sight of God and man.

Proverbs 3:3–4

JUST HELPING OUT

I was teaching my five-year-old daughter, Christine, that God likes us to be helpers. Our home phone number is similar to that of a nearby construction company, so occasionally we get misdirected calls. One morning, when Christine answered one of these calls, I overheard her trying to be helpful. "Well, we don't have construction board," she piped up, "but we do have construction paper."

Diane Thom, Washington

By that same mighty power he has given us all the other rich and wonderful blessings he promised.

2 Peter 1:4 TLB

SUNDAY SCHOOL WIT & WISDOM

GREAT EXPECTATIONS

My three-year-old son, Christopher, memorized his first Bible verse at vacation Bible school: "With God all things are possible." Not much later, we were making plans for the day, and Christopher said, "Let's go to Discovery Zone, the park, the library, and Taco Bell." "That's not possible," I said. "But Mom," he pleaded, "with God all things are possible!"

Carol L. Triebold, Illinois

Whoever keeps doing the will of God will live forever.

1 John 2:17 TLB

GOLD, FRANKINCENSE, AND BILL

While teaching my class of five year olds the story of the Magi and their three gifts, I asked, "Who can name one of the presents?" One little boy excitedly raised his hand and said, "Bill Clinton."

Sherry C. Leavell, Kentucky

All who humble themselves before the Lord shall be given every blessing, and shall have wonderful peace.

Psalm 37:11 TLB

PINT-SIZED BARGAIN HUNTER

After a morning session at vacation Bible school, my grandson, Macky, complained to a friend that there weren't enough red crayons to go around and he only got one cookie at snack time. "Well," said his friend, who remembered their offering, "it really wasn't too bad for a dime."

Aleene Sanders, Missouri

So be truly glad! There is wonderful joy ahead, even though the going is rough for a while down here.

1 Peter 1:6 TLB

DOUBLE-CHECKING

As we returned from vacation Bible school, my young daughter Melissa asked if we could stop at the library. When I asked why, she explained, "This morning my teacher told me the only way we get to heaven is if our name is written in the Lamb's Book of Life. I just wanted to make sure my name is in there!"

Nora Newport, Florida

The Lord has paid me with his blessings, for I have done what is right, and I am pure of heart. This he knows, for he watches my every step.

Psalm 18:24 TLB

PRICELESS RESPONSE

One summer my daughter taught the four year olds at vacation Bible school. The first day she gave everyone yarn necklace name tags to wear. After the recreation time, one little girl, whose name tag had slipped behind her, came running up to my daughter and excitedly proclaimed, "Teacher, teacher, I lost my price tag!"

Sandra Hanson, Minnesota

"My unfailing love for you will not be shaken nor my covenant of peace be removed," says the Lord.

Isaiah 54:10

CLEANUP TIME

It was a great day when my three year old, Kayla, came home from Sunday school and told me she had asked Jesus to come into her heart and wash her sins away. When I told her I was very excited and proud of her, she replied, "Mommy, when Jesus is done cleaning my heart, maybe He'll go in and clean yours too!"

Michelle Bianco, Florida

Neither height nor depth, nor anything else in all creation, will be able to separate us from the love of God that is in Christ Jesus our Lord.

Romans 8:39

PANTS THEOLOGY

My four year old, Michael, raced out the door of his Sunday school room and gave me a big hug. Then he proudly held out a picture he had colored of Jesus and His disciples in flowing robes on the shores of Lake Galilee. "See, Mom," he said, "this is Jesus with His friends." Then he paused and, a bit puzzled, asked, "But how come they don't have any pants on?"

Rae Carmen, Illinois

I will not leave you as orphans; I will come to you.

John 14:18

FEEL IT IN MY BONES

We had recently become Christians, so learning about Jesus was new to our children. Our four year old's Sunday school class discussed asking Jesus into your heart, so on our way home from church, we asked Derek if Jesus was in his heart. He grinned and exuberantly replied, "Not yet—He's in my bones."

Denise Brogan, Kansas

When the Head Shepherd comes, your reward will be a never-ending share in his glory and honor.

1 Peter 5:4 TLB

SHAKIN' THE HOUSE

When recounting the biblical account of the fall of Jericho to my second-grade Sunday school students, I asked, "What do you think made the walls fall down?" "Well," Chad reasoned, "maybe someone played his electric guitar too loud and the vibrations did it."

Lois Akerson, Washington

Give thanks to the Lord, for he is good; his love endures forever.

Psalm 107:1

IN THE BEGINNING

My four-year-old daughter was sharing with me what she had recently learned in Sunday school. "You know what, Mom?" she said excitedly. "God created man; then he took the brain from the man and made woman!"

Laurie Conger, California

I will be your God through all your lifetime, yes, even when your hair is white with age.

Isaiah 46:4 TLB

SHARP HANDWRITING

I was carefully applying the story of Moses receiving the Law to the lives of the four and five year olds in my Sunday school class. I told them that just as God had written with His own finger on the tablets of stone, we could look at the Bible—God's whole written Word—and know exactly how to obey Him and make Him happy. Cutting to the quick, one of my little listeners blurted, "Teacher! God must have sharp fingernails!"

Dawn Waltz, Minnesota

Come here and listen to me! I'll pour out the spirit of wisdom upon you, and make you wise.

Proverbs 1:23 TLB

THIS LITTLE LIGHT

When my husband and I taught two and three year olds in Sunday school, we helped them memorize Psalm 56:3, "When I am afraid, I will trust in You." Our preschool son, Mark, was one of our pupils. One stormy night, as lightning flashed and thunder boomed, the electricity suddenly went off. "I'm not afraid," Mark assured us as we groped in the dark for candles and matches. Expecting him to quote the Bible verse he had recently learned, I proudly prompted him, "And tell us why you aren't afraid." "'Cause I've got my flashlight."

Ann Beck, Mississippi

Let him have all your worries and cares, for he is always thinking about you and watching everything that concerns you.

1 Peter 5:7 TLB

STORYBOOK END

During the children's sermon, the kids were gathered around the pastor discussing the various kings of the world. She showed them pictures of storybook kings and pictures of Jesus. My five year old, Michael, spoke up and said, "Elvis was a king, and he died, just like Jesus."

Carrie Roemmich, North Dakota

The water I give them . . . becomes a perpetual spring within them, watering them forever with eternal life.

John 4:14 TLB

PAID IN FULL

I try to teach my children to give back to God in thanks for our blessings by giving them a quarter for the offering each Sunday. I thought they understood this concept, until a recent episode at the dinner table proved otherwise. During grace, my eight year old thanked God for healthy arms and legs. My nine year old chimed in, "You don't have to thank God for that. We pay Him a quarter every Sunday for that!"

Peggy Williford, Kentucky

I'm going to do a brand new thing. See, I have already begun! Don't you see it?

Isaiah 43:19 TLB

LITTLE LOGIC

I was looking at my three year old's Sunday school papers, which showed the crucifixion of Jesus and the empty tomb. When I asked, "What did you learn about today?" he gave me his usual response: "Jesus." "What about Jesus?" I encouraged. After a short pause he replied very matter-of-factly, "Well . . . He wouldn't stay dead!"

Sue Utesch, Illinois

The reverence and fear of God are basic to all wisdom. Knowing God results in every other kind of understanding. "I, Wisdom, will make the hours of your day more profitable and the years of your life more fruitful."

Proverbs 9:10–11 TLB

PROPHET OR PROFIT?

My son, Scott, and daughter-in-law were teaching third graders in vacation Bible school, and the story for the evening was about Jonah, the prophet. Scott thought it would be wise to explain to the children what a prophet really was, so he first asked them what they thought. Without any hesitation, one little girl responded, "Prophet's what you have left over after you paid all the bills!"

Marilyn J. Hannay, New York

The Lord is my shepherd, I shall not be in want. He makes me lie down in green pastures, he leads me beside quiet waters, he restores my soul. He guides me in paths of righteousness for his name's sake.

Psalm 23:1–3

TAKING CHARGE

No sooner had I deposited my seven year old at her Sunday school class than she reminded me I had forgotten to give her money for the offering. When I told her I'd just emptied my change purse and didn't know how much I could give her that day, she replied, "That's OK, Mom—just give me your credit card!"

Pamela Rubeo, Pennsylvania

Whoever trusts in his riches will fall, but the righteous will thrive like a green leaf.

Proverbs 11:28

THE BEST EVER

In my daughter's vacation Bible school class, the teacher explained to the three year olds that heaven would be better than the most wonderful place they know. My daughter, Erica, quickly raised her hand and excitedly said, "Oh! Then it will be just like McDonald's!"

Jeanne Contreras-Miele, Washington

O my soul, why be so gloomy and discouraged? Trust in God! I shall again praise him for his wondrous help; he will make me smile again, for he is my God!

Psalm 43:5 TLB

NEW TRANSLATION

There are dozens of Bible translations, but Jackie, a vocal six year old, is beginning her own. When her Sunday school teacher asked, "What did David do to Goliath?" she announced, "He wasted him."

Sandy Luraas, New York

The Lord will establish you as his holy people . . . if you keep the commands of the Lord your God and walk in his ways.

Deuteronomy 28:9

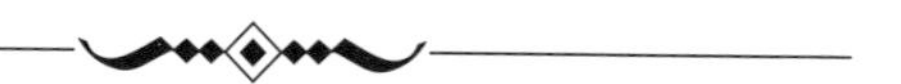

BEST INTENTIONS

I was teaching my young Sunday school class the story of Jesus visiting Mary and Martha. I carefully explained how Martha hurried to clean the house and cook a special meal. Then I paused and asked, "What would you do if Jesus was going to visit your house today?" One little girl quickly responded, "I'd put the Bible on the table!"

Louise Day, Virginia

I pray that as you share your faith with others it will grip their lives too, as they see the wealth of good things in you that come from Christ Jesus.

Philemon 1:6 TLB

SOLID ROCK

At the close of a Sunday school class in which I taught the first and second graders about "building their house on the Rock," I asked one little boy if his house was built on the Rock. He replied, "No. My house is built on wheels!"

Linda Reed, Georgia

All who listen to my instructions and follow them are wise, like a man who builds his house on solid rock.

Matthew 7:24 TLB

IN A CLASS BY HIMSELF

On my most recent visit with my two-year-old grandson, he proudly announced, "I go to Sunday school." "That's wonderful," I told him. "You'll learn about God." He shook his head and insisted, "No, God's not in my class."

Ruth F. Jacobs, Ohio

I am the way and the truth and the life. No one comes to the Father except through me.

John 14:6

DRIVING MR. TRAVIS

I traveled recently from Mesquite, Texas, to Tulsa, Oklahoma, with my three-year-old son, Travis, to visit my parents and attend a seminar at their church. While in the toddler classroom, the caregiver thought she noticed Travis had an accent, so she asked him, "Did you have to drive very far to get here?" He looked at her bewildered and responded, "No, my mom did!"

Jeannia Dykman, Texas

Blessed Lord, teach me your rules. . . . I will meditate upon them and give them my full respect. I will delight in them and not forget them.

Psalm 119:12, 15–16 TLB

Patience, Please!

MIND GAMES

When I baby-sit my minister's three year old, one of our favorite games is Go Fish. One evening, after winning several rounds, she kept bragging about how good she was. Jokingly I said to her, "I'm going to have to teach you a little humility." Immediately she looked up and asked, "How do you play that?"

Orla C. Shup, Pennsylvania

God who began the good work within you will keep right on helping you grow in his grace until his task within you is finally finished on that day when Jesus Christ returns.

Philippians 1:6 TLB

A LION IN SHEEP'S CLOTHING

My son was reprimanding his three year old, Scotty, for spilling food at the table. Little Scotty denied having made the mess. "Scotty, you're lyin'," his dad said. The tot quickly responded, "I not a lion. I Scotty."

Sally Edwards Hayes, Missouri

He holds our lives in his hands. And he holds our feet to the path.

Psalm 66:8–9 TLB

MOUTHING OFF

Winter had caused a nasty case of chapped lips for our four-year-old son, Zachary. After a week of enduring the splitting, bleeding, and peeling skin, he'd had enough. His frustration came through one afternoon as he wearily moaned, "Ooh, I hate when my lips fall off!"

Helen Prater, Michigan

The Lord has compassion on those who fear him; for he knows how we are formed, he remembers that we are dust.

Psalm 103:13–14

MULTIPLICATION TABLES

For morning devotions with my children one day, I read the story about Jesus multiplying the five loaves and two fish to feed a crowd. Later that day, my three-year-old son, Jason, was having difficulty sharing a toy train with his younger sister, Jessica. "Jason," I tried to reason with him, "what do you think Jesus would do?" Not missing a beat, Jason replied, "That's easy, Mom. He'd make two trains out of this one!"

Kathleen Choe, Texas

Whoever has my commands and obeys them, he is the one who loves me. He who loves me will be loved by my Father, and I too will love him and show myself to him.

John 14:21

HEART ANTICS

One afternoon a pregnant friend of mine came to visit. My three-year-old daughter, Annie, was looking intently at my friend's shapely stomach. Noticing her stares, my friend said, "I have a baby in my tummy." Annie replied, "Well, my mommy has Jesus in her heart!"

Nancy Blackshear, Nevada

Be strong and very courageous. Be careful to obey all the law my servant Moses gave you; do not turn from it to the right or to the left, that you may be successful wherever you go.

Joshua 1:7

THORNY THANKS

My son Brant's fourth birthday party was approaching, and I seized the opportunity to work on his manners. I asked, "After you open a gift, what do you say to the friend who brought it?" Immediately he replied, "Thank you." Pleased, I took it a step further. "And what do you say if somebody gives you a toy you already have or a present you don't like?" Without hesitation, Brant proclaimed, "No, thank you!"

Jana Gorham, Oklahoma

Don't be afraid! Speak out! Don't quit! For I am with you and no one can harm you.

Acts 18:9–10 TLB

PULL-OFF ARTIST

My two year old is fascinated with her toy clip-on earrings and never seems to stop asking her father and me to help put them on. One day she started yanking them off only seconds after we'd put them on for her. As she approached her dad for the umpteenth time, he gently took her hands and said, "First, you have to tell me why you pulled them off again." In all innocence, she said, "Why you pulled them off again."

Sherrie Hawthorne, Virginia

Work hard to prove that you really are among those God has called and chosen, and then you will never stumble or fall away.

2 Peter 1:10 TLB

SASSY SEMANTICS

One afternoon I was explaining to our son, Daniel, that God gave us the responsibility as parents to "train" him to obey. Daniel replied, "Mom, training is for dogs. Teaching is for people."

Kathy Gardaphé, Illinois

We are to be kind to others, and God will bless us for it.

1 Peter 3:9 TLB

GOOD POINT

When our children were small, my husband enjoyed taking them in the car whenever he had errands to run. One day four-year-old Michael was seated next to him and asked, "Daddy, what does S-T-O-P spell?" My husband replied, "Stop." Michael asked, "Then why didn't you?"

Cathie McCormick, Pennsylvania

Whoever lives by the truth comes into the light, so that it may be seen plainly that what he has done has been done through God.

John 3:21

PETITE CHEAT

Three-year-old Scottie listened as his mother and her friend discussed playing games. "I cheat when I play games," he stated. Embarrassed that he was admitting this in front of her friend, his mother asked, "Scottie, do you know what happens when you cheat?" "Sure," he said, "I win."

Cheryl Graves, Texas

No temptation has seized you except what is common to man. And God is faithful; he will not let you be tempted beyond what you can bear. But when you are tempted, he will also provide a way out so that you can stand up under it.

1 Corinthians 10:13

BRAINSTORM?

One day while I was student teaching, my cooperating teacher and I asked our students to brainstorm writing topics. One student, after staring at his blank sheet of paper for a few minutes, raised his hand and said, "Miss Diehl, I think I'm having a braindrizzle."

Jennifer L. Diehl, New York

The Lord your God will prosper all you do.

Deuteronomy 15:18 TLB

BROTHERLY LOVE

Although we teach our two boys not to fight, they do get on each other's nerves every once in a while. After one brotherly spat, I asked them to shake hands and then to write each other notes. When they did, rather willingly, I was suspicious. After reading one of the notes, my suspicions were justified: "Daniel to Jon—You better not mess with me, baby, otherwise your name will be mixed up with mud."

Kathy Gnidovic, Illinois

He will give you, through his great power, everything you need for living a truly good life: he even shares his own glory and his own goodness with us!

2 Peter 1:3 TLB

FAST ALIBI

Logan, our preschool son, discovered an unexpected benefit to participating in the church's children's choir. It provided him with a fast out in a moment of brilliance! After issuing a parental command involving his clean-up responsibility, I turned away just in time to hear his little voice respond, "Make me." As I quickly reversed direction to accept his challenge, Logan launched into the chorus of the latest choir song: "Make me . . . a servant today."

Lettie J. Kirkpatrick, Tennessee

The Lord is good, a refuge in times of trouble. He cares for those who trust in him.

Nahum 1:7

PETITE POKES

Our son, Trent, and daughter, Holly, were total opposites in personality. One afternoon, after spending several frustrating hours trying to get Trent dressed, I said to him in exasperation, "Don't be such a slow poke!" Holly evidently was listening, because I heard her say to him later that day, "You're the slow poke." And his response? "Well, you're the fast poke—so there!"

Heather Whitly, California

I will bless you . . . and you will be a blessing to many others.

Genesis 12:2 TLB

MADE TO ORDER

At a church dinner, I took my three young children through the food line. As I juggled everyone's plate and drink, I told the kids to be on their best behavior. When finally seated, I sighed with relief and told them they were doing great—that we hadn't had any catastrophes yet. At that, my three year old, Dawn, looked around and said, "Where are they, Mommy? I'll go get them."

Valerie Kulhavy, Wyoming

Patience develops strength of character in us and helps us trust God more each time we use it until finally our hope and faith are strong and steady.

Romans 5:4 TLB

ASK AND BELIEVE

One day when I was not feeling well, I was telling my granddaughter Melissa, age ten, about my hurting shoulder. She looked at me and said, "Just ask Jesus to fix it. If He made you, surely He can fix you." I thought about it and realized surely He can.

Sue Berry, Texas

I will lie down and sleep in peace, for you alone, O Lord, make me dwell in safety.

Psalm 4:8

HEART CHECK

While waiting in the examination room at the doctor's office, my four-year-old daughter, Hayley, passed time by looking at the wall charts. Her attention was captured by a chart showing multiple views of the heart. When she started to look troubled, I asked what was wrong. With great concern, she replied, "I don't see Jesus in there."

Jeanette Hyatt, California

He reveals profound mysteries beyond man's understanding. He knows all hidden things, for he is light, and darkness is no obstacle to him.

Daniel 2:22 TLB

NICKELS & DIMES

Distressed after numerous attempts to reach her father by a pay phone at the swimming pool, my eight-year-old cousin, Autumn, tearfully asked to use the private phone. Permission was granted, and when Autumn reached her father she explained her distress. "Dad, the phone said use nickels, dimes, or quarters, so I just used a nickel."

Sharon Lundquist, Oklahoma

We live within the shadow of the Almighty, sheltered by the God who is above all gods. This I declare, that he alone is my refuge, my place of safety; he is my God, and I am trusting him. For he rescues you from every trap, and protects you from the fatal plague.

Psalm 91:1–3 TLB

BEDDY BYE

Getting Daniel, our son, to go to bed was a nightly "discussion" for at least a year. During one of those occasions, I finally said in exasperation, "Daniel, I don't want to hear you whine anymore. I'm tired of it." "Then you go to bed," our son promptly responded.

Daniella Johnson, North Dakota

Blessed are the pure in heart, for they will see God.

Matthew 5:8

DISNEY MISSIONARY

As my six-year-old daughter, Amy, sat in the dentist chair to get her teeth cleaned, she started chatting with the hygienist. I overheard Amy say she wanted to be a missionary when she grew up. The hygienist asked if she wanted to go to South America or Africa. Amy thoughtfully responded, "I think I'll go to Disneyland. People need the Lord there too!"

Jan Mullaney, Oregon

The Lord is with you; he protects you.

Proverbs 3:26 TLB

PRACTICE MAKES PERFECT

While waiting in the doctor's office, my son, Allen, and I sat near portraits showing three generations of doctors. Allen studied one picture for quite a while, then asked, "Mom, are those the years he practiced?" I looked at the plaque beneath the picture, which read "Practiced 1907–1954" and said, "Yes, he practiced for forty-seven years." Allen then replied in amazement, "Boy! He sure had to practice a long time before they let him be a doctor!"

Lenita Tosh, Kentucky

Be honest in your estimate of yourselves, measuring your value by how much faith God has given you.

Romans 12:3 TLB

WISHFUL THINKING

As my daughter's fifth birthday approached, friends and relatives asked what she would like for her birthday. Her answer was always the same: "A baby brother." Not wanting her to be disappointed, I told her it took longer than a few weeks for God to make a baby. But if she wanted, she could pray and maybe she would have a baby brother before her sixth birthday. With eyes rolled heavenward and hands on her hips, she stated, "Mom, I don't have to ask God. You just need to eat more so you can get a big tummy!"

Sandy Canout, California

If you want better insight and discernment . . . wisdom will be given you.

Proverbs 2:3 TLB

MATERNAL MALPRACTICE

When Jerome, my friend's five year old, noticed his mother breastfeeding her newborn, he asked her what she was doing. "I'm nursing your sister," she replied. Jerome rolled his eyes and said, "But Mom, you're not a nurse!"

Elise Nacion, Hawaii

Be kind and compassionate to one another, forgiving each other, just as in Christ God forgave you.

Ephesians 4:32

PERSISTENT PERSON

During a family vacation a number of years ago, Jamie, my very persistent younger sister, began to make the usual inquiries that a lengthy car trip with young children seems to bring: "Mom, are we almost there yet?" "How much longer, Mom?" "Mom, when are we gonna be there?" The constant updates on our location finally got to my mother. She turned around and made herself very clear. "Jamie, do not ask me when we will be there one more time. Not one!" Much to our surprise, nearly an hour passed without a single word from Jamie. Then, in her best six-year-old composure, the silence was broken: "Mom . . . how old am I gonna be when we get there?"

Sherry Shiffler, South Carolina

Live as servants of God. Show proper respect to everyone: Love the brotherhood of believers.

1 Peter 2:16–17

BUG LOOK-ALIKE

I once baby-sat for a family where the two year old, Florence, was terribly afraid of any kind of insect. When she was upstairs playing one day, she started screaming, "Bug get me! Bug get me!" I climbed the stairs, preparing to terminate some kind of insect. When I got to the door, I discovered that Florence had been backed into the wall by a stray watermelon seed!

Kim Comer, Georgia

Your attitudes and thoughts must all be constantly changing for the better.

Ephesians 4:23 TLB

"BRIDLE" TACTICS

While on a family outing to a miniature-horse farm, my sister, Paulette, begged Dad to buy her a horse. The fact that we lived in an apartment didn't seem to discourage her from asking. We left for home with Paulette moping in the back of our station wagon. After several attempts to convince Dad that she could keep the horse on our patio and feed it with her allowance money, she was quiet when he asked her how we would get it home. Then, a half hour later, her head popped up over the back seat. "Daddy!" she exclaimed. "We could put roller skates on its feet and tie it to the back of the car!"

Kim Tracey, Ohio

God has already given you everything you need. . . . You belong to Christ, and Christ is God's.

1 Corinthians 3:21, 23 TLB

BETTER NOW?

One Sunday afternoon, my husband, Mike, the children, and I went to a convalescent hospital to sing in their worship service. While there, our boys sang enthusiastically. But as we were leaving, my four year old, Trevor, asked, "Dad, when are we going to the hospital?" Mike replied, "Honey, we were just there." Trevor, confused about this unusual hospital visit, then tenderly asked him, "Well, are you better now?"

Flo Ege, Illinois

But our citizenship is in heaven. And we eagerly await a Savior from there, the Lord Jesus Christ.

Philippians 3:20

GIRLFRIEND WOES

As our family was driving up to the mountains, we were talking about girls with our fifteen year old son and his friends. All of a sudden our eight year old said, "I have a girlfriend—only she doesn't like me."

Mrs. Kevin Viol, California

Let us fix our eyes on Jesus, the author and perfecter of our faith, who for the joy set before him endured the cross, scorning its shame, and sat down at the right hand of the throne of God.

Hebrews 12:2

FAMILY AFFAIR

BATTERIES NOT INCLUDED

My three year old, Evan, watched with great interest as I played with his baby brother, Alan. "Say Mama . . . say Mama . . . say Mama," I playfully begged Alan. After about the third time, Evan became exasperated and explained to me, "He can't talk yet, Mama. He needs batteries."

Lois Hutcherson Jackson, Texas

I will give you new and right desires—and put a new spirit within you.

Ezekiel 36:26 TLB

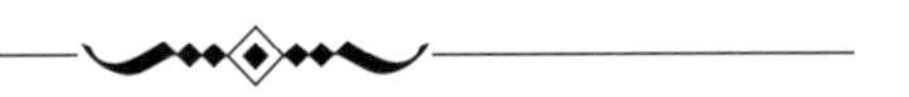

GROWING FEET

When my stepmom visited us recently, she remarked to my five-year-old niece, Jennifer, that she looked like she'd "grown another foot" since they'd last seen each other. Jennifer looked quizzically at her, looked at her own feet, then announced, "No, I didn't! I've always had two feet!"

Sharon Evans, New Mexico

O Lord, you alone are my hope; I've trusted you from childhood. Yes, you have been with me from birth and have helped me constantly.

Psalm 71:5–6 TLB

HAVE A LICK

My two-year-old son, Cody, was eating a Popsicle as my husband, Ken, was on his way out the door. Ken bent down to kiss Cody good-bye, eyed the Popsicle, and asked for a lick. Cody responded by leaning toward his dad and licking him on the cheek.

Danielle Nelson, New York

The Lord your God, the Holy One of Israel . . . has endowed you with splendor.

Isaiah 55:5

DESSERT DYNAMO

One morning as I was preparing to attend a mothers' retreat, my six-year-old son, Tony, asked why I was going. I told him I would learn things to help me be a better mommy. I then asked him if he thought there was anything I could be better at, and he replied, "Yes. Definitely more desserts!"

Carol B. Cuviello, Georgia

[He] redeems your life from the pit and crowns you with love and compassion.

Psalm 103:4

GENETICS GUESS

While in the car on our way to the doctor's office, our four-year-old daughter, Erika, began talking about how much she wanted a baby brother or sister. I told her to keep praying, and maybe someday God would send us one. After several quiet moments, she solemnly asked, "Mommy, if I pray for a baby, is it gonna come in my tummy or yours?"

Debra L. Rokicki, Maryland

No one has ever seen God; but if we love one another, God lives in us and his love is made complete in us.

1 John 4:12

OH, BROTHER!

While pregnant with our third child, I asked our four year old, Shelby, whether she wanted a brother or a sister. She matter-of-factly replied, "I want a sister." When I explained that God might bring her a brother, she responded, "God won't bring me another brother—I already have one!"

Terri E. Kesterke, Washington

I will rejoice in the Lord. He shall rescue me! From the bottom of my heart praise rises to him. Where is his equal in all of heaven and earth?

Psalm 35:9–10 TLB

COMPUTERIZED BABY

In order to help our two-and-a-half-year-old son feel included, my husband and I took him to see the first ultrasound of his developing sibling. On the way home, I asked him what he thought about the baby. He looked concerned, then asked, "Is the baby still in the computer?"

Sonja Waplinger, Pennsylvania

Your light will shine out from the darkness, and the darkness around you shall be as bright as day.

Isaiah 58:10 TLB

FAMILY MIX-UP

The front of our refrigerator is decorated with snapshots: pictures of my children but also a few old wedding pictures. One day when I was straightening some of these, my three-year-old son saw the picture of my father walking me down the aisle and proclaimed, "Mommy, when did you marry Grandpa?"

Paulette Thompson, Pennsylvania

My God will meet all your needs according to his glorious riches in Christ Jesus.

Philippians 4:19

WAKING THOUGHT

When our son, Daniel, was sick one day, I drove home from work to see how he was. When I asked, "How are you doing?" he replied, "Fine, why do you ask?" "Because you were sick this morning," I said, surprised. "Oh," whispered Daniel conspiratorily, "You just thunk I was sick. But I ain't. I've been awake for two weeks!"

Kathy Gardaphé, Illinois

God. . . . has hidden me in the shadow of his hand; I am like a sharp arrow in his quiver.

Isaiah 49:2 TLB

TRADING GAME

When our son, Francis, already a sports lover like his dad, was five, we adopted our baby, Tamara. One afternoon Francis was full of questions. "Where did she come from, Mom?" "From Minnesota," I responded. "Do we get to keep her forever?" he asked. "Yes, she's part of this family—and we wouldn't trade her for anything," I said. Later that afternoon, when Francis was playing with a friend, I overheard him say, "God dropped our baby in Minnesota, and she had to be traded to us. But now we wouldn't trade her—even for a baseball card!"

Tina Thompson, Indiana

I am my beloved's and I am the one he desires.

Song of Solomon 7:10 TLB

BASKET BABY

When our daughter Amy was four, her sister Candee was born. Amy excitedly awaited her arrival home from the hospital, dancing from foot to foot while my husband and I carried into the house the baby and all the gifts we'd received. When we unwrapped Candee from her receiving blanket, Amy stared at her. Then she turned to me and said, "How come she didn't come in a basket like the baby Moses?"

Freda Fisk, Idaho

You saw me before I was born and scheduled each day of my life before I began to breathe. Every day was recorded in your Book!

Psalm 139:16 TLB

LOVE BUGS

When my husband, Daniel, told our three-year-old daughter, Brittany, that some day she and her little sister, Brianna, would be "best buds," Brittany replied, "I'll be the big spider, and Brianna can be the little spider." Daniel was perplexed until he realized Brittany thought she and Brianna would be "best bugs."

Joanne Cornish, Minnesota

Lord, how merciful you are to those who are merciful.

Psalm 18:25 TLB

SPECIAL NEEDS

After praying with Colby, my three year old, I kissed him good night. He asked me to stay with him because he didn't want to be alone. When I reminded him that his younger brother was in the room with him, he responded, "I need a big person." But when I told him Jesus was always with him, Colby pleaded, "But He's a daddy, and I need a mommy."

Debi Matzke, California

Before I formed you in the womb I knew you, before you were born I set you apart.

Jeremiah 1:5

MAID IN HEAVEN

One day I asked my three year old to clean up his room, and he surprised me by posing the very question we'd been teaching him about. "What would Jesus do?" I stammered, "Well . . . I guess He'd clean it." To which my son quickly responded, "Get Him to do it, then!"

Michelle Stewart, Ontario

The Lord is fair in everything he does, and full of kindness.

Psalm 145:17 TLB

DON'T LOSE MAMA!

My daughter, Doris, and her children were staying with us for a few weeks. One day four-year-old Laura and I dropped Doris off at the hair salon. As we drove on, I jokingly said, "I guess we can find this place again." Laura looked concerned and said, "I'll help you, Grandma." At each corner, Laura pointed a thumb in the direction we came from. But after three turns she gave up and said, "I hope you can find her, Grandma—because if you don't, my daddy will be mad!"

Janice Kramar, California

My justice and mercy shall last forever, and my salvation from generation to generation.

Isaiah 51:8 TLB

LOGICAL EXTENSION

Gabriel was six when his brother was born, and he was present for the birth. The experience must have made quite an impact because yesterday, when our TV plug wouldn't reach the socket, he asked me, "Mommy, don't you have an umbilical cord?"

Cheryl Stewart, Michigan

You have been loving and kind to me and will be to my descendants.

Psalm 18:50 TLB

JOY ON THE JOURNEY

Four-year-old Zachary had been going through a difficult stage. In a moment of extreme exasperation, I asked him, "Zachary, what am I going to do with you?" I stopped in my tracks and had to say a prayer of thanks when he replied, "Enjoy me!"

Cheryl Stewart, Michigan

My grace is sufficient for you.

2 Corinthians 12:9

A WAKING SLEEP

When five-year-old Sara continued to wake me up several times during the night for small things such as a drink of water or finding her teddy, I told her not to wake me up for such trivial things because I needed my sleep. She replied, "God does not get any sleep." With a long sigh, I said, "Honey, I'm not God. I'm just your mom. And I need *my* sleep!"

Annette Vroegh, Illinois

He gives food to those who trust him; he never forgets his promises.

Psalm 111:5 TLB

SEEKING SANCTUARY

Right before our family vacation, my husband and I decided to transfer our children from a Christian school to a public one. While traveling, our seven-year-old daughter, Andrea, announced that she needed to use the bathroom. When we stopped at a gas station, my husband went in to inquire about their facilities but returned to explain they didn't have any public rest rooms. Desperately Andrea pleaded, "Oh, Daddy, please go ask if they have any Christian ones!"

Pierrette M. Begent, New York

The righteous will never be uprooted, but the wicked will not remain in the land.

Proverbs 10:30

A TWINKLE IN HER EYE

Our three-year-old son, Joshua, was talking with his dad about our wedding picture. Joshua asked where he and his younger brothers were when the picture was taken. My husband told him they were just a twinkle in their mother's eye. Joshua looked perplexed and asked, "How could she see with all those twinkles!"

Carolyn Cuany, North Carolina

The eyes of the Lord are intently watching all who live good lives, and he gives attention when they cry to him.

Psalm 34:15 TLB

WOMB ACTIVITY

When I was eight-and-a-half months pregnant, my four-year-old daughter asked, "Mommy, where was I when you were a little girl?" I responded, "Well, you were in my thoughts." A few moments later she asked, "Where are your thoughts?" I answered, "My thoughts are in my head." She thought another moment, then declared, "Oh, I see—babies scoot from your head to your tummy!"

Barbara Neale, Virginia

Those who are wise will shine like the brightness of the heavens, and those who lead many to righteousness, like the stars for ever and ever.

Daniel 12:3

BUTTERING UP DAD

On a camping trip with the family, my husband searched the motor home for butter to melt over the popcorn. "Where's the butter? Who hid the butter?" he kept muttering to himself, loud enough for the rest of us, sitting outside, to hear. Finally he yelled out to our daughter, "Judi! Where's the butter?" Judi answered back, "How would I know, Dad? Am I your butter's keeper?"

Ila Mason, California

How wide and long and high and deep is the love of Christ.

Ephesians 3:18

SUPER STRIPPER

My four year old was playing outside with the water hose, sprinkling the lawn and filling a small tub. I checked on her periodically and later found her with no clothes on. I went to her immediately and said, "June, honey, we never take our clothes off outside." In all sincerity, she answered, "Oh, I didn't. I took them off in the basement."

Edna Caudill, Ohio

Surely this is our God; we trusted in him, and he saved us. This is the Lord, we trusted in him; let us rejoice and be glad in his salvation.

Isaiah 25:9

S-E-X

One day, as my husband and I were getting into the car with our eight-year-old son, he asked, "Dad, what is sex?" I shot a look across the car at my husband that said, *I'm glad this one is yours!* He returned my look with shock. Then he asked our son, "Why do you want to know?" To which he replied, "Well, the other day I saw this piece of paper that said, 'SEX Male Female.' What does that mean?" We sighed in unison.

Leanne Goff, Nebraska

In your strength I can scale any wall, attack any troop.

Psalm 18:29 TLB

ACCIDENTS DO HAPPEN

When my son, Paul, was in kindergarten, he came home and proudly shared the memory verse he'd learned. "Honor thy father and thy mother. Accidents 20:12."

Toni Friesen, California

If my people, who are called by my name, will humble themselves and pray and seek my face and turn from their wicked ways, then will I hear from heaven and will forgive their sin and will heal their land.

2 Chronicles 7:14

FOR MEN ONLY

As our five year old, Molly, watched her daddy pack for a Promise Keepers weekend, she asked, "Daddy, can I go with you?" My husband explained the weekend was only for men. Molly mused, "Is it like a men's bathroom?"

Beth Hugdahl, Illinois

As for those who serve the Lord, he will redeem them; everyone who takes refuge in him will be freely pardoned.

Psalm 34:22 TLB

BEING UP FRONT

When our daughter was born, our young son was upset because he wasn't able to help feed her. My husband told him he could watch Mommy so he would understand why only I could feed Elisa. At the hospital he stood and watched me nurse her. Afterwards he leaned over and asked me seriously, "How long do you have to wear those?" "Wear what?" I responded. "Those things you feed the baby with."

Dori Goebel, North Carolina

I am living and strong! I look after you and care for you. I am like an evergreen tree, yielding my fruit to you throughout the year. My mercies never fail.

Hosea 14:8 TLB

HOPELESSLY DEVOTED

Shortly after our family began having nightly devotions—which isn't easy with a precocious four-year-old daughter and an impish two-year-old son—my daughter asked, "Mommy, when are we gonna get together with Daddy and Austin to talk about God and have family commotions?"

Carla Crumley-Forest, Florida

For the Lord God is a sun and shield; the Lord bestows favor and honor; no good thing does he withhold from those whose walk is blameless.

Psalm 84:11

WEDDING BELL BLUES

My husband had taken his first pastorate and had an approaching wedding to perform. The bride was a member of our church, and for several weeks our children heard comments about Daddy marrying Amie. Our five year old became depressed. With each passing day, her usually bubbly personality faded, and I became concerned. I pulled her into my lap one day and asked why she wasn't happy. In a burst of tears, she sobbed, "I love Daddy, and I don't want him to marry Amie!"

Doris Marie Mataya, Washington

Guard your affections. For they influence everything else in your life.

Proverbs 4:23 TLB

IN THE RIGHT PLACE

During my second pregnancy, we often spoke to our three-year-old son, Alec, about "the baby in Mommy's tummy." One day my husband was talking about how Jesus can live in our hearts and asked if Alec would like to have Jesus in his heart. "No," Alec confidently replied. "I'd like Him in my tummy!"

Lisa M. Casto, Ohio

I will remember the deeds of the Lord; yes, I will remember your miracles of long ago. I will meditate on all your works and consider all your mighty deeds.

Psalm 77:11–12

BOOMERANG SINS

After a particularly frustrating day with three-year-old brother Brett, his exasperated sister, Caitlyn, stated, "You know, Mom, God must have given Brett all his sins back."

Jan Buscher, Illinois

A life of doing right is the wisest life there is.

Proverbs 4:11 TLB

STILL LOVE YOU

One morning while I was putting on my makeup, my three year old discovered an old high school picture of me. He brought it to me and asked, "Who's this lady?" I answered, "That's me when I was real young." "Oh," he pondered, then wondered aloud, "Did I still love you then?"

Lezlie M. Winberry, California

Blessed are they who keep his statutes and seek him with all their heart.

Psalm 119:2

THROUGH THE ROOF

Our three-year-old, Wade, had developed the habit of tattling on his brother, Louis, who had just turned one, and we told him to stop. One day when I was driving to the grocery store and both boys were in the backseat, Wade asked, "Mommy, can God see through the car roof?" "He sure can," I answered. "Well, then," he continued cautiously, "can He see Louis back here taking all the Kleenexes out of the box?"

Linda Hamilton, Nevada

You are a chosen people, a royal priesthood, a holy nation, a people belonging to God, that you may declare the praises of him who called you out of darkness into his wonderful light.

1 Peter 2:9

MINT?

My young son and his grandmother were walking the few blocks to our grocery store when he trotted ahead of her. She called for him to come back, because trying to keep up with him was causing her to be "out of breath." His reply was, "Don't worry, Grandma, my mom's got plenty of breath mints in her purse."

Jean Hudson, Illinois

Surely goodness and love will follow me all the days of my life, and I will dwell in the house of the Lord forever.

Psalm 23:6

IT KEEPS GOING . . . AND GOING

I didn't realize how modernized our three-year-old grandson T.J. was until one day when he was visiting. We were sitting on the floor, and I was trying unsuccessfully to get our three-month-old foster baby to coo and talk. Reaching over and lifting the baby, he looked at her back, then said to me, "The baby can't talk. She doesn't have any batteries."

Frances J. Hutson, North Carolina

Show proper respect to everyone.

1 Peter 2:17

FIRST THINGS FIRST

I recently had Bethany, my second baby, and my mother was telling my five-year-old brother, Jared, about baby Bethany's relationship to him. "Now you have a nephew and a niece!" Mom told Jared proudly. To that Jared replied, "But I thought I needed a wife first."

Dawn Ryan, New York

It is best to listen much, speak little, and not become angry.

James 1:19 TLB

FRECKLES FOR TWO

Our daughter, Taylor, has a light sprinkling of freckles across her face. When asked where she got them, she always replies, "My daddy gave them to me!" (Her daddy is generously covered with freckles from head to toe.) One afternoon, I found her staring at her face in the mirror. "What are you looking at?" I asked. "At how many freckles I have," she answered. "I don't think Daddy shares very well!"

Sandra Bacon, Arizona

The name of the Lord is a strong tower; the righteous run to it and are safe.

Proverbs 18:10

Memory Mania

I CAN DO ALL THINGS . . .

One evening at dinner, C.J., my five-year-old nephew, covered his cantaloupe with catsup. Kimberly, his sister, looked at him incredulously and asked how he could eat this combination. Proudly he announced, "I can do all things through Christ who strengthens me!"

Julie Kroneman, Washington

Don't be anxious about tomorrow. God will take care of your tomorrow too. Live one day at a time.

Matthew 6:34 TLB

A HIGHER ORDER

Tired of struggling with my strong-willed three-year-old son, Thomas, I looked him in the eye and asked a question I felt sure would bring him in line: "Thomas, who is in charge here?" Not missing a beat, our Sunday-school-born-and-bred toddler replied, "Jesus is."

Susan C. Kimber, California

The Father himself loves you because you have loved me and have believed that I came from God.

John 16:27

SCRIPTURE MIX-UP

When my daughter was quite young, we would sit and cuddle in the big recliner every night before bed and read Bible stories. One night she wanted to read to me: "Jesus was a good shepherd, he led his flocks to the green pastries."

Marjory Kasen, North Carolina

If you fully obey the Lord your God and carefully follow all his commands I give you today, the Lord your God will set you high above all the nations on earth.

Deuteronomy 28:1

FOR PETE'S SAKE

When my son, Danny, was four years old, I started to teach him the Twenty-third Psalm. Every time he recited a verse correctly, he received a coin for his piggy bank. One day, he was trying to earn a coin for the third verse and said, "He leadeth me in the paths of righteousness for Pete's sake."

Jan Buhr, Michigan

He lets me rest in the meadow grass and leads me beside the quiet streams. He restores my failing health. He helps me do what honors him the most.

Psalm 23:3 TLB

THE CHEESE WHO STANDS ALONE

One evening, as three-year-old Kayla was getting ready for bed, she began naming the people she wanted to pray for. In her list, she included "the cheese." Her mother asked who "the cheese" was, and Kayla was shocked that her mom didn't know it was "the cheese who stands alone."

Dawn Elgie, New York

God will open wide the gates of heaven for you to enter into the eternal kingdom of our Lord and Savior Jesus Christ.

2 Peter 1:11 TLB

NOTHING TO SNEEZE AT

I frequently use 1 Thessalonians 5:17 to encourage the children I teach to "pray without ceasing." One day after chapel, a young boy said, "Mrs. Capehart, I'm sorry I sneezed during your prayer today." I assured him sneezing was no problem, but I appreciated his apology. He responded, "Well, I know you like us to pray without sneezing."

Jody Capehart, Texas

He humbles the proud and brings the haughty city to the dust; its walls come crashing down. He presents it to the poor and needy for their use.

Isaiah 26:5-6 TLB

MAY EYE HELP YOU?

My sister, who has diabetes, was explaining to her four-year-old daughter, Taylor, and three-year-old son, Alex, what to do in an emergency. Trying to keep it simple, she told them to call 911 and tell the operator, "My mommy has diabetes." When she quizzed them to see if they understood, Taylor responded correctly, and Alex answered, "I call 911 and say my mommy has beady eyes."

Cheryl Spinks, Texas

The Lord is faithful, and he will strengthen and protect you from the evil one.

2 Thessalonians 3:3

CREATIVE BOWLING

After several hectic years with three small children under the age of five, my husband and I agreed we needed a "date night" for just the two of us every month. Just before we headed out the door on our first date, I explained we were going bowling and that the baby-sitter would take care of them while we were gone. Five-year-old Samuel raced into the kitchen and came back with one of my mixing bowls on his head. "But, Mom—see, I could go bowling too!"

Linda Nutell, North Dakota

He will teach the ways that are right and best to those who humbly turn to him.

Psalm 25:9 TLB

HOW ROMANTIC

My five-year-old son, Joshua, learned the first six books of the New Testament in Sunday school. He proudly recited them to me after church, "Matthew, Mark, Luke, John, Acts, Romantics!"

Kyongmi Odell, New Hampshire

For it is God who works in you to will and to act according to his good purpose.

Philippians 2:13

BIBLE VEGETABLES

A little girl returned home from Sunday school and proudly announced that she had memorized a new Bible verse. "Eat carrots for me," she recited. Her confused mother called the Sunday school teacher for an explanation. She discovered that the verse was 1 Peter 5:7 (KJV): "He careth for me."

Dolores Ritter, Nebraska

Find rest, O my soul, in God alone; my hope comes from him. He alone is my rock and my salvation; he is my fortress, I will not be shaken.

Psalm 62:5–6

MATERIAL WORLD

I was reminded of our culture's focus on the exterior the other day when my five-year-old daughter tried to recite a verse she'd learned. With great pride, she voiced Matthew 5:16, "Let your light shine before men that they may see your good looks and praise your Father in heaven."

Linda Rogalski, California

The Angel of the Lord guards and rescues all who reverence him.

Psalm 34:7 TLB

ARMOR OF GOD

My daughter Mercy asked me why her daddy didn't wear his seat belt in the car. Before I could answer, she interjected, "I know why! It's because he has on the armor of God!"

Colleen Monaghan, Pennsylvania

Put on the full armor of God, so that when the day of evil comes, you may be able to stand your ground, and after you have done everything, to stand.

Ephesians 6:13

YANKEE DOODLE DANDY

My great nephew, Jaren, loves to pretend he's a pastor. My niece stands outside his room and listens as he opens his Bible and delivers a sermon. Her favorite so far was when Jaren concluded with, "Jesus rode into town on a donkey, stuck a feather in his hat, and called it macaroni."

Rita Howard, Georgia

Jehovah is kind and merciful, slow to get angry, full of love.
Psalm 145:8 TLB

GIVE US LORD OUR JELLY BREAD

When Shawn, our eldest, was old enough to say grace before meals, we taught him the traditional mealtime prayer, "God is great; God is good . . ." He quickly learned the words and was delighted to give the mealtime blessing. We soon found ourselves chuckling, however, for he concluded with his own version of this well-known prayer: "and give us Lord our jelly bread." Now Shawn is seven; his brother, Daniel, is five. They take turns offering the blessing, and daily bread remains jelly bread.

Brenda L. Reed, Pennsylvania

I am the Bread of Life. No one coming to me will ever be hungry again. Those believing in me will never thirst.
John 6:35 TLB

SCRIPTURE SHORTS

My two and a half year old, Emily, has been enjoying her "Hide 'em in Your Heart" album by Steve Green. She listens to it over and over. Recently we realized she had memorized some of the Scripture verses she'd been hearing on the album when she referred to her shorts as her "shorts of the Glory of God!"

Martha Matzke, Texas

The Lord grants wisdom! His every word is a treasure of knowledge and understanding. He grants good sense to the godly.

Proverbs 2:6–7 TLB

SHIRLEY GOODNESS

One afternoon, I was reading a picture book of the Twenty-third Psalm to our three-year-old daughter, Natasha. The illustration for "Surely goodness and mercy shall follow me all the days of my life" depicted three little children near a shepherd. As I finished reading the book, Natasha asked, "Mommy, which one is Shirley?"

Tamara Hill, Indiana

Let us please God by serving him with thankful hearts.

Hebrews 12:28 TLB

GOD TALK

WHAT BIG EYES YOU HAVE!

When my toddler and I were at the mall one day, an older woman made a comment about how beautiful my daughter's eyes were. Then the woman bent down and asked her, "Where did you get those big beautiful eyes?" Without missing a beat, my daughter confidently replied, "From God, silly!"

Kathy Carter, Alabama

For this God is our God for ever and ever; he will be our guide even to the end.

Psalm 48:14

DISCIPLES EXPANDED

Flipping through our children's Bible, I pointed to a picture of Jesus surrounded by His disciples and asked my daughter to explain the story in her own words. Looking at it, she said, "Mommy, this is a story about Jesus. And here are all His disciples—Matthew, Mark, Luke, John, Acts, and Romans!"

Nena Jurek, Texas

The Lord says, "I will make my people strong with power from me! They will go wherever they wish, and wherever they go, they will be under my personal care."

Zechariah 10:12 TLB

HELPING HAND

My three-year-old cousin, Mark, accidentally spilled his fruit punch on the floor. He decided to clean up the mess himself and dashed to the back porch to get the mop. Suddenly realizing it was dark outside, he became apprehensive about reaching out the door for the mop. When his mother reminded him that Jesus is everywhere—even in the dark—Mark thought for a moment. Then, putting his face to the door, he called, "Jesus, if You're out there, will You hand me the mop?"

Kathy Gunter Martin, Tennessee

Consider it pure joy, my brothers, whenever you face trials of many kinds, because you know that the testing of your faith develops perseverance.

James 1:2–3

JACK OF ALL TRADES

There was a period of time when our family car was giving us quite a bit of trouble. As I was starting it to take my son, Jack, to school one day, I stopped to pray. When Jack asked me what I was doing, I explained that Jesus helps those who pray. With an incredulous expression, he said, "But Mommy, Jesus isn't a gas station man, is He?"

Joan Brodie, New York

Be of one mind, united in thought and purpose.

1 Corinthians 1:10 TLB

PULLED IT OFF SINGLE-HANDEDLY

My young grandson, Richard, and I recently vacationed in the Rocky Mountains. One day we had stopped to admire their grandeur, and after a few minutes of thoughtful silence Richard broke out, "Just think—God did all this with only one hand!" I puzzled over this for a moment, then asked him what he meant. "Oh, you know, Grandmother," he replied, "the Bible says Jesus was sitting on the right hand of God!"

Mrs. Harvey Kidd, Mississippi

The Lord is wonderfully good to those who wait for him, to those who seek for him.

Lamentations 3:25 TLB

JUNIOR REVELATION

My eight-year-old daughter, Cali, chose to rent a six-hour video about Jesus from our church library. After watching about two-thirds of it over the next few days, she came to me with what seemed to be a new revelation to her. "I know who Jesus is!" she announced. "God, Junior."

Robin Searles, Minnesota

Train a child in the way he should go, and when he is old he will not turn from it.

Proverbs 22:6

COLORFUL IMAGINATION

My nieces Jessica, age five, and Stephanie, age three, were chatting with their mom when Stephanie asked, "Mommy, does God really make rainbows?" "Of course He does," my sister replied. Jessica nudged Stephanie and explained, "Only God has such big crayons."

Shirl Cooke, Pennsylvania

He is the image of the invisible God, the firstborn over all creation. For by him all things were created. . . . He is before all things, and in him all things hold together.

Colossians 1:15–17

KNOCK, KNOCK

Our pastor's five year old eagerly went to a neighbor's house to return a borrowed item, but he returned in minutes with the item still in hand. With disappointment in his little voice, he reported, "No one was home but God—and He didn't answer the door."

Linda K. Sproull, Indiana

I am leaving you with a gift—peace of mind and heart! And the peace I give isn't fragile like the peace the world gives. So don't be troubled or afraid.

John 14:27 TLB

PLAY BALL!

At a recent trip to the golf driving range, our five-year-old son, Austin, was watching his father hit golf balls. As a particularly high shot was in the air, Austin looked at me with awe. "Wow, Momma," he said. "That ball is so high that Jesus could catch it."

Sharron Cook, Michigan

Because of his kindness you have been saved through trusting Christ. And even trusting is not of yourselves; it too is a gift from God.

Ephesians 2:8 TLB

TWINKLE, TWINKLE, LITTLE STAR

My five-year-old, Daniel, and I were contemplating why God made so many stars, most of which we cannot see without a powerful telescope. I suggested, "Maybe God made them to show us how big He is." Then Daniel added, "Or how small we are."

Kathy Gnidovic, Illinois

By one sacrifice he [Jesus Christ] has made perfect forever those who are being made holy.

Hebrews 10:14

MIGHTY MAKER

We had been teaching our two-year-old daughter, Kali, that God is the Creator who made all things. One morning, after I made her bed, she climbed back into it to play. "Hey," I said, "I just made that!" "No, no," Kali replied, "God made it!"

Brenda Stearns, California

When we obey him, every path he guides us on is fragrant with his lovingkindness and his truth.

Psalm 25:10 TLB

HOW DO YOU SPELL BELIEF?

My four-year-old nephew, Michael, is just learning how to spell. We were spending the day together when he suddenly blurted, "My mom knows about a lot of things, Aunt Kath, but there's one thing she just doesn't know." "What's that, Michael?" I inquired. "She says Jesus and God are the same." "And why don't you think that's true?" With great authority he declared, "Because Jesus and God don't spell the same!"

Kathy Richardson, Michigan

Though I am absent from you in body, I am present with you in spirit and delight to see how orderly you are and how firm your faith in Christ is.

Colossians 2:5

SOMEONE IS WATCHING

My four-year-old daughter, Kaitlyn, wanted to climb up into her older sister's bunk bed to use it as her pretend tree house. "I'm sorry, Kaitlyn," I said, "but you are not allowed in the upper bunk unless someone is watching you." "But Mom!" she protested, "Jesus is watching me!"

Lynette Kittle, Florida

I am but a pilgrim here on earth: how I need a map—and your commands are my chart and guide.

Psalm 119:19 TLB

BREATH OF GOD

One sweltering summer night, my grandkids stayed overnight. When two-year-old Sarah finally fell asleep in my bed, six-year-old Nick and I headed for the deck to cool off. We sat together in the twilight, enjoying the ocean breeze that swept through the nearby apple orchard and fir forest. "Isn't God good to give us this breeze to cool us off!" I said. Nick snuggled next to me and added, "And doesn't God's breath smell good!"

Billie Mazzei, Washington

If we endure, we will also reign with him.

2 Timothy 2:12

NIGHT VISION

I overheard my daughters talking in the hallway. Stephanie was telling her younger sister Michelle, "Don't turn the light on in that room because nobody will be in there." Michelle reasoned, "God is—He's everywhere." Stephanie quickly answered, "Yeah, but He can see in the dark."

Penny L. Shemory, Pennsylvania

Teach me to do your will, for you are my God; may your good Spirit lead me on level ground.

Psalm 143:10

SEEK AND YE SHALL FIND

My three-year-old Joshua and I were talking one night before bed. I told him Jesus is always with us wherever we go, and He'll never leave. Quite some time later when I thought he was asleep, I peeked into his room to find Joshua leaning over his bed, fishing around under it as if to find something. He looked up and said, "I know He's under here somewhere!"

Jill Baldwin, Idaho

Call to me and I will answer you and tell you great and unsearchable things you do not know.

Jeremiah 33:3

WHOSE HOUSE?

My family is close friends with another family who faithfully attends our church. Often we spend Sunday afternoons together relaxing at our house. One day when I phoned these friends, their four-year-old daughter, Alicia, answered and politely asked who was calling. To tease her, I said kiddingly, "Alicia, you come to my house almost every Sunday and you don't know who I am?" In a reverential voice, she replied breathlessly, "Jesus?"

Stacy Penalva, Indiana

Whoever hears my word and believes him who sent me has eternal life.

John 5:24

THE GREENHOUSE EFFECT

Our daughter Maegan was just learning about spiritual matters. When I explained that she could ask Jesus to live in her heart and make a home for Him there, she enthusiastically announced, "Yea, I'm going to make Him a greenhouse!"

Rhonda Hover, Kansas

It is God who arms me with strength and makes my way perfect. He makes my feet like the feet of a deer; he enables me to stand on the heights.

Psalm 18:32–33

BE STILL, MY HEART

While working as a nanny, I spent a lot of time talking about my faith with my four-year-old charge, Jackie. One day he told me he wanted to become a Christian. I explained what it meant and how wonderful it was to be a Christian. He eagerly invited Jesus into his heart. Later that week, I found him giggling hysterically as he jumped up and down on his bed. More curious than angry, I asked, "Jackie, what are you doing?" He answered, "I'm making Jesus dizzy!"

Christine O'Donnell, Virginia

The fruit of the Spirit is love, joy, peace, patience, kindness, goodness, faithfulness, gentleness and self-control.

Galatians 5:22–23

"HANDY" CAPPED

When my four-year-old nephew was being taught about Jesus' being in heaven, sitting at the right hand of God, he asked his mother, "Why does Jesus sit on His right hand? He'd get more done if He used both hands!"

Lori Beezhold O'Dea, Illinois

The Lord has made the heavens his throne; from there he rules over everything there is.

Psalm 103:19 TLB

HAIL EXCITEMENT

My sister, Phyliss, was baby-sitting her four-year-old granddaughter, Kirsten, when it began to rain. They quickly ran onto the porch, but not before hail began to fall. As the golf-ball-sized bits of ice began to bounce on the ground, Phyliss said, "Look, Kirsten, it's hail. That's little pieces of ice falling." Kirsten, who had never seen hail before, got excited. "I didn't know Jesus could do that!"

Donna C. Smith, Tennessee

You have a wonderful future ahead of you. There is hope for you yet!

Proverbs 23:18 TLB

GROWN-UP WISDOM

During my six years of nannyhood I was fortunate enough to be able to communicate the gospel to the children in my care. I wanted to emphasize the love Christ has for children, so I taught them songs such as "Jesus Loves the Little Children" and "Jesus Loves Me." I guess I focused a little too heavily on Jesus loving children, for when five-year-old Angela was singing "Jesus Loves the Little Children," she stopped suddenly, looked at me seriously, and asked, "Does Jesus love grown-ups too?"

Deana Galang, California

We love because he first loved us.

1 John 4:19

ALL IN THE FAMILY

While running errands with my three-year-old niece, Charity, I probed her understanding of God by asking her who He is. She screwed up her face in deep thought, then grinned as she filled me in: "God is Jesus' father-in-law."

Becky Arnold, Arkansas

We are saved by faith in Christ and not by the good things we do.

Romans 3:28 TLB

HEAVENLY HUMOR

MOVIN' ON UP

When my son, Jeffrey, was three, he asked a lot of questions about spiritual matters. Shortly after his grandpa died, he started pressing us on how God gets people up to heaven. "Mom," he asked intently, "does God drop a rope or ring the doorbell?"

Barbara Spurlock, California

Jehovah himself is caring for you! He is your defender.

Psalm 121:5 TLB

CLOUD HOPPING

I finished the lesson on Jesus' return by asking my toddler class what they'd learned. One little boy frantically waved his hand high. As soon as I called on him, he blurted out, "When Jesus comes down from heaven on the cloud and gets real close, I'm gonna hop on!"

Ellie Banas, Illinois

God makes us ready for heaven—makes us right in God's sight—when we put our faith and trust in Christ to save us.

Romans 1:17 TLB

DESTINATION UNKNOWN

One morning my four-year-old son, Kevin, and his grandpa went out to buy donuts. On the way, Grandpa turned to Kevin and asked, "Which way is heaven?" Kevin pointed to the sky. "Which way is hell?" Kevin pointed toward the floor of the truck. Grandpa continued, "And where are you going?" "Dunkin' Donuts," Kevin replied.

Kathy Chapman, Florida

I sought the Lord, and he answered me; he delivered me from all my fears.

Psalm 34:4

HEAVENLY WEAR

I was browsing in the ladies' section of a local store with my son who was just learning to read. Trying to read all the signs he could, he came upon one in the maternity department. "Look, Mom!" he said excitedly as he pointed at the sign. "They're even making clothes for eternity now!"

Norma Lauby, California

Whoever listens to me will live in safety and be at ease, without fear of harm.

Proverbs 1:33

HIGH FLYING

Our four-year-old son, Cody, and his father were riding back from town. Cody was quiet for a while, then brightened up and shared an insight: "Daddy, I know why God made the clouds so high! So the birds won't bump their heads!"

Becky Smith, Tennessee

Your promises are backed by all the honor of your name.

Psalm 138:2 TLB

CHEF JESUS

During a weekend trip to the mountains, Scotty's father asked him what he thought God was doing in heaven. Scotty replied, "God's cooking dinner." Probing further, his dad asked, "What do you think God is cooking?" Before Scotty could answer, his older brother, Ryan, jumped in, "Daddy, he's cooking the Last Supper!"

Ora Lee Anderson, Virginia

Whatever you do, work at it with all your heart, as working for the Lord, not for men, since you know that you will receive an inheritance from the Lord as a reward. It is the Lord Christ you are serving.

Colossians 3:23–24

UP, UP, AND AWAY!

During Easter season, I told our children a different story about Jesus each night: about His birth, about His ministry, His triumphal entry, His trial, death, and resurrection. On the final night, I told them that Jesus was alive, that He would be coming back to take us up to heaven someday, and that we'd be able to see way above the clouds. "Oh, goody!" six-year-old Shelly replied. "Is He coming in an airplane?"

Carmen Coniver, Montana

You will be filled up with God himself.

Ephesians 3:19 TLB

CONFUSED FACTS

Alice, age six, was sitting beside me in the car as we drove past a cemetery. She pointed out the window and said, "There's heaven." Puzzled, I asked her what she meant. "Well, that's where people go when they die, so it must be heaven."

Kirtes Calvery, Missouri

The Lord is faithful to all his promises and loving toward all he has made.

Psalm 145:13

HEAVENLY PARTY

When my grandfather was told he had only a few months to live, our daily prayers always included special petitions for him. Now that he's passed on, our six-year-old daughter, Kathleen, continues to pray for him. But now her prayer goes like this, "Dear God, please bless Great-Grandpa so that he's having a good time in heaven."

Joan Marie Arbogast, Ohio

This is the confidence we have in approaching God: that if we ask anything according to his will, he hears us. And if we know that he hears us—whatever we ask—we know that we have what we asked of him.

1 John 5:14–15

HEAVE HO

My husband taught in a Christian school for many years. One student, in writing a brief testimony for an assignment, misspelled the word *heaven*. She wrote, "When I die, I am going to heave."

Jan Buhr, Michigan

He will cover you with his feathers, and under his wings you will find refuge; his faithfulness will be your shield and rampart.

Psalm 91:4

CAN IT WAIT?

One Wednesday after our children's club meeting, our family stopped at Dairy Queen. It was a special evening because our four year old had just asked Jesus into her heart. My husband, wondering how much she actually understood, asked her, "So you want to go to heaven to see Jesus?" "Yes," she replied. "But can I finish my Dilly Bar first?"

Tammy McBee, Illinois

Jesus replied. . . , Those the Father speaks to, who learn the truth from him, will be attracted to me."

John 6:43–45 TLB

BEDTIME PRIORITIES

Our bedtime routine with our three-year-old Annie is to read a book, say our prayers, and go to bed. One day I explained to Annie that when we get to heaven, we won't have to pray anymore because we'll just talk to Jesus face to face. Later that week, I overheard her imparting her wisdom to her father: "Daddy, when we get to heaven, we won't have to pray anymore. We'll just read a book and go to bed!"

Kim Reade, Kansas

Stand at the crossroads and look; ask for the ancient paths, ask where the good way is, and walk in it, and you will find rest for your souls.

Jeremiah 6:16

TAGGED IN HEAVEN

One day while visiting my father's grave with my five-year-old granddaughter, Christina, we began talking about heaven. She said she'd been wondering about the number of people there. Curious, she asked, "Will we wear name tags?"

Donna Seller, New York

I will turn their mourning into joy and I will comfort them and make them rejoice.

Jeremiah 31:13 TLB

TROUBLE IN THE RANKS

My grandson, Joshua, an inquisitive seven year old, asked, "Grandma, did you know they kicked the devil out of heaven?" "Yes, Joshua," I answered, "I'd heard that." To which he replied, "Well, I wish they hadn't done that, cause he's caused us an awful lot of trouble."

M. Joan Miller, Indiana

I will call upon the Lord to save me—and he will. I will pray morning, noon, and night . . . and he will hear and answer.

Psalm 55:16–17 TLB

GOING TO SEE THE KING

After weeks of hospitalization and heroic efforts by her doctors, our premature baby, Laura, died at three months. A few days later, I was rocking two-year-old Rachel when she sighed and said, "I'm so glad Laura died." We'd spent a lot of time with Laura over the past months, and I'm sure Rachel felt a little neglected, but I whispered, "I'm sad Laura is gone. Why are you glad?" She answered with great understanding and compassion, "Because now she's with Jesus and is so happy!"

Sharon R. Hamatake, Utah

In my Father's house are many rooms; if it were not so, I would have told you. I am going there to prepare a place for you.

John 14:2

HEAVEN ON EARTH

While leaving our small-town carnival, our sons, ages six and two, were walking hand-in-hand behind my husband and me. We overheard Tyler tell his younger brother, Cory, "This is what heaven is like—except it's free!"

Sandra Cox, Indiana

Lord, I am overflowing with your blessings, just as you promised. Now teach me good judgment as well as knowledge.

Psalm 119:65–66 TLB

KODAK MOMENT

One hot summer evening, my husband and I took our three-year-old daughter, Tara, outside for some fresh air. The dark sky lit up as an electrical storm began a brilliant show. Tara broke our silence when she provided the reason for the phenomenon. "Look, Daddy! Jesus is taking pictures of us!"

Christy L. Truax, Virginia

I am the light of the world. Whoever follows me will never walk in darkness, but will have the light of life.

John 8:12

FACTORY FUN

Our four-year-old foster son, Michael, and I were traveling to the store. As we passed by a factory smokestack belching out billows of white smoke, Michael said, "Oh, so that's the factory where clouds are made!"

Debbie Harter, Ohio

Don't you know by now that the everlasting God, the Creator of the farthest parts of the earth, never grows faint or weary? No one can fathom the depths of his understanding. He gives power to the tired and worn out, and strength to the weak.

Isaiah 40:28-29 TLB

BLONDE WISHES

When six-year-old Katie learned of her grandmother's death, friends and family explained that one receives a new body in heaven. "Good," Katie responded, "because when I go to heaven, I'd like blonde hair."

Kathleen Hicks, Tennessee

I lift up my eyes to you, to you whose throne is in heaven.

Psalm 123:1

LANDLUBBER

One December day, five-year-old Emily noticed that our perpetual calendar was still showing November, so she asked to change it. As she rearranged the numbers, she asked if we had any birthdays in December. With a grin, I said, "Yes, one on December twenty-fifth." She cocked her head and said, "Nooooo, someone we know." I said, "We do know someone whose birthday is celebrated December twenty-fifth." She stamped her foot and said, "No, no, no! Someone who lives on land!"

Lynn M. Roberts, Florida

Treat others as you want them to treat you.

Luke 6:31 TLB

COUNTDOWN

Our three oldest children were being interviewed for church membership. The elders questioned them about their understanding of grace: "If Jesus had never come and died on the cross, is there any other way you could get to heaven?" My six-year-old son, Stephen, jumped in, "Yes! By spaceship!"

Dottie Free, Pennsylvania

The name of the Lord is a strong tower; the righteous run to it and are safe.

Proverbs 18:10

PASSING ACQUAINTANCE

When we visit my parents' grave site, my boys always help water the flowers. One day they argued over who should get to water. Knowing my youngest was born one month after my father died, my elder son said, "You can't do it. You didn't even know Grandpa." To that my little one replied, "Oh, yes, I did. I was coming down when he was going up."

Elsie Ratowski, Michigan

Let us practice loving each other, for love comes from God and those who are loving and kind show that they are the children of God, and that they are getting to know him better.

1 John 4:7 TLB

CLOUDY VISION

Our family recently flew to England. As we ascended into the clouds, my six-year-old son, Nicholas, stared wide-eyed out the window. Suddenly he yelled, "I think I see God!"

Renae Brobst, England

They will be my people, and I will be their God.

Ezekiel 11:20

MAP READING 101

A friend of mine was running errands with her daughter. The young girl was studying a road map intently. Suddenly she shook her head and remarked, "Mom, this map isn't right. I can't find heaven on it anywhere."

Susan Dolle, Indiana

Just as the mountains surround and protect Jerusalem, so the Lord surrounds and protects his people.

Psalm 125:2 TLB

THE BIG CLIPPER

Late one night our family went out for a boat ride on the lake. My six-year-old son, Brian, gazed up at the partial moon and said, "Mommy, look! God's fingernail must have fell off!"

Mari Kay Watson, Tennessee

God will tenderly comfort you when you undergo these same sufferings. He will give you the strength to endure.

2 Corinthians 1:6–7 TLB

HOT ROD TO HEAVEN

My four year old and I were talking about Jesus when she asked if she'd ever get to see God. I told her that one day Jesus will come and take us home with Him, and then we'll get to be with God. She thought again and asked, "What color car will Jesus be driving?"

Debbie Hammers, Kentucky

I will betroth you to me in faithfulness and love, and you will really know me then as you never have before.

Hosea 2:20 TLB

EYE IN THE SKY

Leaving church one Sunday night, our three-year-old daughter, Cassidy, noticed some lights streaming through the sky. As we drove, my husband and I explained that spotlights were on to draw attention to some particular store or event in town. After listening to our explanation, Cassidy asked me, her voice full of wonder, "Mommy, are the lights tickling God?"

Yvette Johnson, Georgia

In repentance and rest is your salvation, in quietness and trust is your strength.

Isaiah 30:15

STARRY SKIES

My husband and I took our two children to a planetarium. While sitting in the dark theater gazing up at the stars, the four year old, Stephen, became perplexed and asked, "But Mommy, when do we get to see God?"

Shirley Bartone, Ohio

Blessed are those who hunger and thirst for righteousness, for they will be filled.

Matthew 5:6

HIGHWAY TO HEAVEN

On a recent vacation, our six-year-old daughter, Amanda, spotted a large picture of Christ captioned "Are you on the right road?" She asked, "Dad, are we on the right road?" When we explained that Jesus is asking if we are on the right road to heaven, not Canada, Amanda bounced out of her seat and excitedly asked, "We're going to heaven? Do I have enough clothes?"

Vicky McCristal, Michigan

This is my prayer: that your love may abound more and more in knowledge and depth of insight.

Philippians 1:9

BLACK AND BLUE

When our family experienced the death of my grandmother, our daughter, Elizabeth, six, started asking a lot of questions. One night before sleep, she asked, "Mom, when people die, do they have their eyes closed?" I explained that when you sleep, you close your eyes, but then you open them again when you wake up. But when you die, you don't open your eyes again. At that last statement, she looked rather confused and said, "That's crazy. Everyone in heaven will be bumping into each other!"

Lori Richards, Indiana

Whatever a person is like, I try to find common ground with him.

1 Corinthians 9:22 TLB

A MAILBOX IN HEAVEN?

My three-year-old daughter, Jordan, recently lost both maternal great-grandparents. One day she handed me a very colorful drawing. "For me?" I asked. "No, Mommy. I'm going to mail this to Great-Grandma and Great-Grandpa," she replied. When I tried to explain to her that they both lived in heaven with Jesus, she stated adamantly, "I know. I'm going to mail them to Jesus' mailbox in heaven!"

Melissa Hamby, North Carolina

Let us consider how we may spur one another on toward . . . good deeds. Let us . . . encourage one another.

Hebrews 10:24–25

BLACKOUT

Since our church was only a couple of blocks away, it was our habit to walk to church. One Sunday night, our three-year-old John, finding it rather dark, looked up into the sky. Seeing no stars, he said disappointedly, "Oh, no stars. God turned them off!"

Susan P. Ayers, Georgia

Lord, help me to realize how brief my time on earth will be. Help me to know that I am here for but a moment more.

Psalm 39:4 TLB

HOLIDAY MOMENTS

MOO TESTAMENT

While helping my five-year-old twins rehearse "Away in a Manger" for their Christmas concert, I struggled to explain the lyrics. "The cattle are lowing . . . " When I told them that people spoke differently in Old Testament times than they do today, my daughter, Robin, piped up, "Old Testament cows low—and New Testament cows moo!"

Kathie Erwin, Florida

You believe in him and are filled with an inexpressible and glorious joy, for you are receiving the goal of your faith, the salvation of your souls.

1 Peter 1:8–9

DIVINE REVELATION

When my daughter lost her last baby tooth, I was weary of the Tooth Fairy and decided it was time to dispel this childhood myth. "Kelli," I said, "you know how the Easter Bunny is really Mommy, and Santa Claus is too?" "Yes," she replied, a bit warily. "Well, there's one more person who is really me. Can you guess who that is?" Slowly Kelli's eyes grew as big as saucers, and her mouth dropped open. In a small, awe-filled voice, she said, "God?"

Ellen Yinger, Ohio

The Lord watches over all who love him.

Psalm 145:20

SPELLING BEE

I asked my seven-year-old niece, Melissa, if she had done anything special to celebrate Valentine's Day. "Yes," she said, "I got lots of Valentine cards from the kids at school. And the one from Brian said, 'To Melissa, Love Brian.'" "Wow," I responded. "Do you think he loves you?" "Oh, no," she assured me. "He doesn't know how to spell from."

Susan Voth, British Columbia

Blessed is the Lord, for he has shown me that his never-failing love protects me like the walls of a fort!

Psalm 31:21 TLB

NESTING INSTINCTS

As my mother and I strolled with my three-and-a-half-year-old son, Brandon, through the Christmas section of a department store, we stopped to look at a beautiful nativity scene. Brandon eagerly pleaded with my mother to hold "the baby Moses." Explaining to him that it was the Baby Jesus, not the baby Moses, she gently lifted the figurine from the manger and handed it to him. Not yet content, he said, "No, Granny, I want to hold His nest too."

Carla Talley, Arkansas

Kind words are like honey—enjoyable and healthful.

Proverbs 16:24 TLB

SHADOW PLAY

My three-year-old son, Logan, was just beginning to learn about the holidays we'd celebrate in the months ahead. After Valentine's Day, he asked, "When is Easter, Mommy?" I told him. "Goody!" Logan said. "I can't wait to hunt for Easter eggs!" I reminded him, "Remember what Easter is all about? Remember how Jesus rose from the ground?" "Oh, yeah," my incredulous son replied. "And He didn't see His shadow!"

Lori Kragt, Michigan

[God] is able to do immeasurably more than all we ask or imagine, according to his power that is at work within us.

Ephesians 3:20

MIXED APOLOGY

Our son, Daniel, and his cousin, Jodie, decided to talk to each other through the clothes chute. So Daniel went upstairs, and Jodie went downstairs to the basement. On the spur of the moment, Daniel decided to surprise Jodie, and he spit down the clothes chute, hitting Jodie in the face. When Jodie came up to the kitchen and told us what happened, I made Daniel apologize. He did, very willingly: "I'm sorry I spit on you." Then, sweetly, thirty seconds later, he added, "I should have thrown water instead."

Daniella Johnson, North Dakota

The more we undergo sufferings for Christ, the more he will shower us with his comfort and encouragement.

2 Corinthians 1:5 TLB

NO ROOM AT THE INN

When I was five and a half, my parents took our family to Death Valley in our travel trailer for Christmas vacation. My grandparents decided they would like to join us but stay at the Death Valley Inn. When my grandmother called and informed us that there was no room at the inn, I told my mother, "Then why can't they stay in the manger?" In my young mind, if it was good enough for Jesus and His family, certainly it would be good enough for my grandparents.

Janine Dueck, California

You are my friends, proved by the fact that I have told you everything the Father told me.

John 15:15 TLB

ALL IS CALM

As our family was eating dinner one evening before Advent, I asked, "Who can tell me what the four candles in the Advent wreath represent?" Luke, my seven year old, exuberantly began, "There's love, joy, peace, and . . . and . . . " Eager to keep up with her brother, six-year-old Elise excitedly broke in, "I know! Peace and quiet!"

Michelle Hardie, Michigan

You will lie down in peace and safety, unafraid.

Hosea 2:18 TLB

FACT OF ORIGIN

At Thanksgiving, our two-year-old granddaughter was being quizzed on where things come from. She told us that turkey meat came from turkeys, chicken meat came from chickens, and ham came from pigs. Then we asked where hamburger came from, and without hesitation she filled us in. "From McDonald's."

Sally Johnson, Illinois

Great is his faithfulness; his lovingkindness begins afresh each day.

Lamentations 3:23 TLB

SEASON OF WONDER

Arriving at a friend's home for a Christmas party, my four-year-old daughter, Megan, noticed the illuminated, life-size nativity scene decorating the front yard. She immediately dropped to her knees on the icy lawn, reverently clasped her mittened hands, and bowed her head before the manger. Watching her almost took my breath away. We should all be in such childlike awe of the blessed Babe.

Cindie Masui, California

Set your minds on things above, not on earthly things.

Colossians 3:2

TO DYE FOR

My three-year-old Rachel and I were dyeing Easter eggs at Grandma's house. We talked about what colors we would use, then Grandma told her to put the eggs in the cups so they would dye. After a few minutes of watching these colorful creations in the making, Rachel looked up and asked, "Grandma, do you think those eggs are dead yet?"

Teresa Saueressig, Kansas

You are a forgiving God, gracious and compassionate, slow to anger and abounding in love.

Nehemiah 9:17

HOLIDAY HAND-ME-DOWNS

The Sunday before Christmas, my Sunday school class brought me gifts. One little girl presented her package and innocently said, "Here, someone gave this to my mommy, and she didn't want it."

Alison Denight, Florida

You will go out in joy and be led forth in peace; the mountains and hills will burst into song before you, and all the trees of the field will clap their hands.

Isaiah 55:12

LEOPARDS IN CHURCH?

For Thanksgiving, our church's youth group put on a play about gratitude, performing the story of the ten lepers. Although all were healed by Christ, only one returned to express his thanks. On the way home, my seven-year-old daughter announced, "That was a good story, wasn't it?" "Which story was that?" I asked. "You know," she replied. "The one about the ten leopards."

Laurie Beithan, Washington

Listen to advice and accept instruction, and in the end you will be wise.

Proverbs 19:20

MARY WHO?

My three year old was delighted with the Christmas créche I had bought for her. As we carefully assembled it, I explained the story of Mary, Joseph, and Baby Jesus. I wanted to make sure she understood what the scene was all about, so I asked her to repeat the story for me. Very proudly she said, "I know!" and started singing, "Mary had a little lamb, little lamb, little lamb . . . "

Diane Spicer, New York

Let us hold unswervingly to the hope we profess, for he who promised is faithful.

Hebrews 10:23

COME ON ALONG

As we prepared for our church Easter egg hunt, I decided it was time to explain to my three year old, Patti, the meaning of Easter. I told her Jesus died on the cross to pay for our sins and then came back to life after three days—so we celebrate Easter because Jesus is alive. She thought for a few seconds and asked, "Is He coming to the Easter egg hunt today?"

Tina Mitchell, Arkansas

Gladness and joy will overtake them, and sorrow and sighing will flee away.

Isaiah 35:10

BIG GULP

While teaching my fours-and-fives class the Christmas story, I reached the part about Baby Jesus lying in the manger. My son, Dale, wanting to impress his friends, blurted out, "I know what Baby Jesus was dressed in—swallowing clothes."

Christine Armstrong, South Carolina

You were there while I was being formed in utter seclusion! You saw me before I was born and scheduled each day of my life before I began to breathe. Every day was recorded in your Book!

Psalm 139:15–16 TLB

IN JESUS' LAP

At age two, my daughter enjoyed seeing Santa Claus and the Easter Bunny in the mall. However, she was always afraid to sit in their laps. Shortly after Easter, she asked, "Mommy, is God real?" "Yes," I replied. "Good," she rejoiced. "When He comes to the mall, I'm going to sit in His lap."

Ginger Horn, Alabama

He tends his flock like a shepherd: He gathers the lambs in his arms and carries them close to his heart; he gently leads those that have young.

Isaiah 40:11

MARY AND LARRY

As Christmas approached, my husband and I spent a great deal of time discussing Baby Jesus, Mary, and Joseph with our two-year-old daughter. While taking a walk one day, we noticed our neighbor Larry drive by and waved. "Look, Natalyn," I said, "there's Larry." "Yeah," she replied, "and Joseph!"

Autumn D. Meinardus, Texas

Those who hope in the Lord will renew their strength. They will soar on wings like eagles; they will run and not grow weary, they will walk and not be faint.

Isaiah 40:31

WHY HE ROSE

When my daughter, Sarah, was four years old, I asked her to explain the meaning of Easter to our relatives gathered around the table. She enlightened us by saying, " . . . And on the third day, He rose from the tomb to hide all the Easter eggs!"

Christine Bushman, Illinois

Before long, the world will not see me anymore, but you will see me. Because I live, you also will live.

John 14:19

CAN YOU KEEP A SECRET?

My four-year-old John was helping me wrap Christmas presents for his daddy. When we finished, he said, "Now let's wrap some presents for me." I told him, "Oh, no. I want your presents to be a surprise." He quickly assured me, "But I won't tell myself!"

Tammy Heinrich, Texas

You are indeed God, and your words are truth; and you have promised me these good things. . . . Bless me and my family forever!

2 Samuel 7:28–29 TLB

GESUNDHEIT!

As my young children and I left the mall after a day of Christmas shopping, the three year old asked if he could put some money in the Salvation Army bucket. After he dropped in his money, the bell ringer smiled and said, "God bless you." Instantly my son looked confused and asked me, "Did I sneeze?"

Kim Duncan, Alaska

I will instruct you and teach you in the way you should go; I will counsel you and watch over you.

Psalm 32:8

READY AND WAITING

While driving to church on Easter Sunday, I told my children the Easter story. "This is the day we celebrate Jesus' coming back to life," I explained. Right away, my three-year-old son, Kevin, piped up from the backseat, "Will He be in church today?"

Peggy Key, Michigan

Everything comes from God alone. Everything lives by his power, and everything is for his glory.

Romans 11:36 TLB

JAM SESSION

One Sunday evening I overheard my five-year-old daughter, Julie, practicing "Hark, the Herald Angels Sing," a song she'd been rehearsing that morning in church for next week's Christmas program. It was all I could do to suppress my laughter when, in place of "with angelic host proclaim," Julie sang, "With the jelly toast proclaim."

Marilyn Clark, Ohio

Whatever is good and perfect comes to us from God, the Creator of all light, and he shines forever without change or shadow.

James 1:17 TLB

A GIFT FROM GOD

I gave my nephew, Jonathan, a Bible for Christmas. Because it was wrapped in plastic, I wasn't able to fill out the "Presented to . . . From . . . " page. But Jonathan had no problem with that. He just filled it out himself: "Presented to . . . Jonathan. From . . . God."

Amy Gaston, Pennsylvania

There is none like the God of Jerusalem—he descends from the heavens in majestic splendor to help you.

Deuteronomy 33:26 TLB

A ROSE BY ANY OTHER NAME . . .

After months of coaching, my young daughter finally seemed to understand that Jesus died to take away our sins. I moved on to the next lesson and started telling her, "Jesus was buried, but after three days arose and went to heaven." She looked me straight in the eye and asked, "What does a rose have to do with it?"

Janiee Knapp, New York

In this world you will have trouble. But take heart! I have overcome the world.

John 16:33

A BEARY MERRY CHRISTMAS

Every year our family selects a tree from a local tree farm. When my son, Donnie, was three, he could hardly contain his excitement. As we set out through the fresh morning snow, I warned the kids to avoid "bare spots" in choosing a tree. Donnie grew quieter and quieter as we walked through the trees. That night I understood why, when he prayed, "And thank You, God, for no bears today at the tree farm!"

Deborah Brooks, Michigan

The Lord will keep you from all harm—he will watch over your life; the Lord will watch over your coming and going both now and forevermore.

Psalm 121:7–8

A REAL LIVE NATIVITY

My sister-in-law's church presented a live nativity scene as part of a Christmas service devoted to children. The voice of a preschooler rose from the audience, "Look, Mama! There's Baby Jesus on His changing table!"

Lisa I. Poole, Washington

The Lord delights in you and will claim you as his own.
Isaiah 62:4 TLB

LITTLE LESSONS

ON THE EDGE

When my daughter Katie was a toddler, she worried about falling off the changing table. Twisting her head so that the end of the table was right in front of her eyes, she would cry, "I fallin', Mama! I fallin'!" When my reassurances would fail, I'd say, "Don't look at the edge. Look at Mama." As her focus shifted to my face, she would become peaceful. I, too, know the temptation to "look at the edge" when unpredictable or difficult times arise. Again and again God must remind me, "Look at Me, daughter. Don't look at the edge." How sweet it is to lift my eyes to meet His faithful and loving gaze and know peace in the midst of turmoil.

Nita Landis, Pennsylvania

Cast your cares on the Lord and he will sustain you; he will never let the righteous fall.

Psalm 55:22

HEADACHE CURE

My son, Jared, woke me up one night complaining of a bad headache. After giving him some Tylenol, I made him a bed on the floor in our room and tucked him in. Seconds later, he was standing beside our bed again. "Mom, can we pray?" I was humbled. I thought I'd taken care of all his needs, yet I'd neglected his spiritual need. His faith inspired me.

Roxane McCoskey, Iowa

I am holding you by your right hand—I, the Lord your God—and I say to you, Don't be afraid; I am here to help you.

Isaiah 41:13 TLB

HOW TIME FLIES

My youngest son, Austin, posed an interesting question: How many days had we lived on this earth? The answer was astonishing. I'd lived 12,502 days, and he'd lived 2,234 days. I recalled Psalm 90:12, "Teach us to number our days. . . ." Truly our days are precious. I pray I'll fill them with kindness and love—and teach my children to do the same.

Ruth-Ann Williams, Michigan

God did not give us a spirit of timidity, but a spirit of power, of love and of self-discipline.

2 Timothy 1:7

THE BIG NURSERY

When my daughter, Carly, was almost two, she decided she'd had enough of nursery life. As I left her in the nursery one day, she said, "You know, Mom, I'd much rather go to the Big Nursery!" I stopped in my tracks and thought, *How many times do I view Sunday morning worship as a nursery to entertain me, instead of seizing the wonderful opportunity to express love and devotion to my Creator?*

Tamara Hough, West Virginia

God chose from the very first to give you salvation, cleansing you by the work of the Holy Spirit and by your trusting in the Truth.

2 Thessalonians 2:13 TLB

A STILL, SMALL VOICE

It was an exasperating morning. Our phone rang constantly, I washed a contact lens down the drain, our dryer died, and our dog, Princess, sat on the deck and barked incessantly. My head reeled. "Anna, please go tell Princess to be quiet," I told my daughter. "But Mom," she pleaded, "Princess is singing 'Jesus Loves Me'—I just know it!" What I considered noise, my daughter saw as one of God's creatures praising Him. Cheered, I realized I don't have to be inside a peaceful sanctuary to learn from Him. I just have to be listening.

Dayle A. Shockley, Texas

When you pray, I will listen.

Jeremiah 29:12 TLB

STUCK IN A RUT

"Help, Mommy!" yelled my two year old as she struggled to dress herself. When I rushed to help her, I found her arm stuck through the neck hole of her blouse. But she refused to let go of the shirt, making it impossible for me to correct the situation. I realized I sometimes treat God the same way. Now when I pray, "Help, God!" I try to let go of my preconceived solutions. God might have different plans—but I'll only hinder His work if I continue to clutch mine.

Connie Holman, Florida

If two of you on earth agree about anything you ask for, it will be done for you by my Father in heaven.

Matthew 18:19

TRUST

Eager to share his new knowledge, my six year old proudly announced, "I know what's on all the U.S. coins." "What?" "In gold we trust," Ryan said with a big smile. Our family chuckled a little as I explained that the motto was In God We Trust. Later I kept thinking about "in gold we trust." Ryan's version was more accurate, I realized. Too often I put more faith in my material possessions than in the Lord who provides them.

Carol McFarland, Virginia

The Lord will open the heavens, the storehouse of his bounty, to send rain on your land in season and to bless all the work of your hands.

Deuteronomy 28:12

SWEET FLAVOR

My husband's sister-in-law has a music time with the prekindergarten/kindergarten children that I teach during our church's midweek program. One night, while the kids were learning the words to a song, she asked, "What is a Savior?" One child responded, "Some kind of candy . . . you know, Lifesavers!" Although we chuckled at the time, a short while later we realized that the child was right. Jesus really is our "Life Savior!"

Deanna Emmert, Oregon

For the wages of sin is death, but the gift of God is eternal life in Christ Jesus our Lord.

Romans 6:23

THE MIND OF A CHILD

At bedtime I tuck in my four-year-old daughter, Kaitlyn, pray with her, and kiss her good night. I pray that God will protect her mind at night so she won't have any nightmares. One night I wasn't feeling well so I asked Kaitlyn if she would tuck me into bed. She pulled up my covers and took my hand to pray with me. At the conclusion of her prayer, she said, "And God bless Mom with Your mind." Her sweet childish words impacted my heart and held great wisdom: someday we will all have the mind of Christ.

Lynette Kittle, California

And we know that all that happens to us is working for our good if we love God and are fitting into his plans.

Romans 8:28 TLB

HOME, SWEET HOME

Upon returning home from a business trip, my husband, Dave, was greeted by warm hugs and kisses. While he unpacked his bags, our young daughter wrote a note and taped it to the bathroom mirror. It said: "I missed you. I am glad you came back. I miss you vary vary vary much." Dave beamed when he read the note. And I couldn't help but think that God must feel like that when the wayward come home to Him.

Joan Marie Arbogast, Ohio

The eyes of all mankind look up to you for help.

Psalm 145:15 TLB

SIMPLE JOYS

One morning when my daughter was two, I heard her chattering and playing in her crib. I opened her door to get her up for the day and was met with the biggest, brightest smile and one excited word: "Jesus!" Now, whenever my life becomes consumed by the world and worries around me, I think of that morning. It reminds me of how Jesus told us to be childlike. What a lesson of joy and simplicity I learned from my child that day!

Cathy Blake, Colorado

Do not let your hearts be troubled. Trust in God; trust also in me.

John 14:1

A CHILD'S FAITH

We had recently purchased the book *When God Doesn't Make Sense*, by James Dobson, and our seven-year-old son, Colin, noticed it lying on the counter. He read the title and proclaimed, "Mom! God always makes sense! It's just that you don't understand Him!" Heavenly Father, teach us to have such childlike faith, to trust in Your perfect plan.

Christine Graham, Virginia

Even when we are too weak to have any faith left, he remains faithful to us and will help us . . . and he will always carry out his promises to us.

2 Timothy 2:13 TLB

PASS IT ON

My faith was given a boost when my daughter's kindergarten teacher told a story about her. On the last day of school, each child was asked to make a wish for her classmates. While most wished, "Have a good summer," my daughter said, "I wish all my friends would have Jesus in their hearts."

Julia L. Corbin, Ohio

Commit to the Lord whatever you do, and your plans will succeed.

Proverbs 16:3

A FISTFUL OF "DANIEL-LIONS"

"Happy Mutter's Day, Mommy!" my three year old exclaimed as he handed me a fistful of dandelions. "They're beautiful," I replied. Then he proclaimed with a grin, "They're Daniel-Lions." "You mean dandelions," I corrected him. "No, Mommy," he insisted. "I like to call 'em 'Daniel-Lions.'" All summer long on my kitchen counter sat a small vase filled with bunches of Daniel-Lions. They were a constant reminder for me to pray that my three little sons would be bold like Daniel—never afraid to speak freely of their God.

Deana Rogers, Nevada

What a wonderful God we have—he is the Father of our Lord Jesus Christ, the source of every mercy, and the one who so wonderfully comforts and strengthens us in our hardships and trials.

2 Corinthians 1:3–4 TLB

SPREADING THE WORD

As I was cleaning the kitchen, I secretly wished my precious Lauren would take a break from her constant conversation. Amid her stream of questions she asked, "Mommy, if people are born, and alive, but they don't know Jesus and are not born again, does that make them the living dead?" I paused in my work and answered, "Yes, I suppose it does." She became excited and decided we needed to start telling everyone in the neighborhood about Jesus. So we turned up the stereo and sang praise songs out the kitchen window at the top of our lungs. I'm sure Lauren thought the whole world heard. I know Jesus did.

Vera Ann Folden, Washington

The Lord is close to those whose hearts are breaking; he rescues those who are humbly sorry for their sins.

Psalm 34:18 TLB

KISSES FROM HEAVEN

My daughter, Robyn, called me at work to send kisses over the phone. "Here they come!" I excitedly replied to her smooching noises. With childish wonder she asked, "Mom, did my kisses go through the telephone, up to heaven, and then down to you?" What a revelation—our love for others touches the heart of God before reaching them.

Brenda R. Ulman, Maryland

The Lord loves justice and fairness; he will never abandon his people. They will be kept safe forever.

Psalm 37:28 TLB

JESUS SAID YES

Just before the start of the fireworks celebration, I spoke quietly to my three year old, "I'll hold you during the fireworks. If you think you might be scared, pray for Jesus to help you." Seconds later he replied, "Jesus said yes." Not only was his prayer answered, but he clapped and shouted when it was over. Fears—we all have them. Jesus says yes to us too.

Cathy Walker, Illinois

Don't be afraid, for the Lord will go before you and will be with you; he will not fail nor forsake you.

Deuteronomy 31:8 TLB

A CALL AWAY

My friend's five-year-old daughter was spending the night with me. In the middle of the night, she sat up in bed and called my name. When I responded, she said, "I just wanted to know you're here." She promptly lay down and went to sleep again. It occurred to me how comforting it is—even as an adult—to know Jesus is with me anytime, day or night.

Laura Ament Peck, Colorado

You can get anything—anything you ask for in prayer—if you believe.

Matthew 21:22 TLB

THE STRONG ARM OF GOD

My brother and I were preparing to leave the bank with his five-year-old daughter, Melissa. She ran ahead to open the heavy door. She huffed, puffed, and pushed. She stepped back and started again. Finally she pushed with all the might her little body could muster—and the door opened. She was unaware that her father's hand, high above her head, had actually pushed the door open for her. I laughed but then realized God does the same for me every day.

Vicky Marra, Ohio

Praise God for the privilege of being in Christ's family and being called by his wonderful name!

1 Peter 4:16 TLB

OUT OF THE MOUTHS OF BABES

I was delighted one Saturday morning to awake to the smell of waffles cooking and the sound of my two small boys chattering with my husband. I sat on my husband's lap and gave him an affectionate hug and thank-you for the extra needed hours of sleep. Later that day, he and I were having a heated discussion when we stopped mid-sentence. Our son, Jacob, stood in the doorway. He looked at me, and, with as much authority as a four year old can muster, said, "Mommy, try to remember how you felt when you were on Daddy's lap!"

Jane Schmidt, Oregon

Each one of you also must love his wife as he loves himself, and the wife must respect her husband.

Ephesians 5:33

A HIGHER CALLING

My long hours working as a child-care provider often tempted me to complain about my job. Although I didn't know what work God wanted me to do, I was sure it must be something other than just baby-sitting. Then one day, a father who came to pick up his toddler commented, "You taught Kasey to pray. She says grace at home now, and my wife and I are thinking of attending church." God's direction suddenly became clear. Now, when others ask what I do for a living, I smile and say, "I 'just' baby-sit for the Lord."

Linda Clare, Oregon

He that winneth souls is wise.

Proverbs 11:30 KJV

LEARNING CURVE

I occasionally bake cookies with my two nieces. Usually they want to do most of the work themselves, even though it would be much faster if I did it. I was getting impatient with them one day, when I thought of our heavenly Father looking down on us. He lets us do things ourselves. It takes us longer than if He just did it for us, but that's how we learn.

Jo-Ann M. Hansen, New York

Have faith and love, and enjoy the companionship of those who love the Lord and have pure hearts.

2 Timothy 2:22 TLB

RETURN TO SENDER

When my niece, Toni, turned six, I excitedly gave her some gifts I had spent extra time shopping for. Two weeks later, when I asked if she was enjoying them, I was disappointed to learn she had decided to return some of them. Even after my careful selection of those gifts—intended especially for her—she hadn't really appreciated them. As I asked God to help me get over my disappointment, I remembered some of the gifts He had given me—gifts that I hadn't appreciated either and wished I could have exchanged for others.

Patti Greenman, Missouri

Devote yourselves to prayer, being watchful and thankful.
Colossians 4:2

TEETER TOTTER

I watched my son walk toward me for the first time. He teetered this way and that and fell many times—but he was walking! It made me reflect on my first steps of faith. I, too, teetered and tottered and fell many times. But just as I found much joy in my son's accomplishment, how great must my heavenly Father's joy have been as I began my journey toward Him.

Cynthia Sturtz, Iowa

Teach me your way, O Lord, and I will walk in your truth.
Psalm 86:11

A CROWN OF SPLENDOR

My young son concluded that my gray hair was like a dried-up pen, needing a "refill." I decided to color my hair. As I awaited my "new look," I happened to read Proverbs 16:31: "Gray hair is a crown of splendor; it is attained by a righteous life." I'd been so concerned about going gray that I'd forgotten God looks at my heart. Just as my silvery "crown" will return, without continual "refills," my heart will run dry without a daily refill from God.

Linda Clare, Oregon

As for God, his way is perfect; the word of the Lord is true. He shields all who hide behind him.

2 Samuel 22:31 TLB

IN HIS NAME

While in nursery school, my daughter Aimee would bring home drawings with the name of someone she loved next to her own name. "I did this for you," she'd proudly say. As Scripture says, "Whatever you do . . . do all in the name of the Lord Jesus" (Colossians 3:17). If Aimee could do every school project for me or for her dad, surely I can do all my "projects" for my heavenly Father. Now I often ask myself, "Have I written my Lord's name on all I have done today?"

Laura DuVall Bush, Connecticut

We can be mirrors that brightly reflect the glory of the Lord. And as the Spirit of the Lord works within us, we become more and more like him.

2 Corinthians 3:18 TLB

HE'S GOT ME COVERED

One night while my young son, Ryan, was sleeping, a storm began brewing. After a loud clap of thunder, I heard Ryan wake up and run to find me, so I headed toward his room to comfort him. When I tucked him back into bed, he asked me to stay with him until he fell asleep. As I lay there with him, I realized Ryan hadn't asked me to make the storm go away but to stay with him. How many times, I wondered, have I asked God to take away the storms of life when, instead, I need to ask Him to stay with me and help me weather the storms more peacefully!

Kim Sherer, Oklahoma

The wise in heart are called discerning, and pleasant words promote instruction.

Proverbs 16:21

Acknowledgments and Permissions

To each of the authors who allowed us to reprint their stories in this book, we extend our grateful thanks:

"On Her Own" Copyright © Karen Aaker
"Shakin' the House" Copyright © Lois Akerson
"Moonstruck" Copyright © Lynne Allen
"Pet Preference" Copyright © Shawntel Allen
"Last Meal" Copyright © Kay Ammon
"Humpty Dumpty" Copyright © Carole Anderson
"Chef Jesus" Copyright © Ora Lee Anderson
"A Very Special Garden" Copyright © Debbie Andreasen
"Heavenly Party" and "Home, Sweet Home" Copyright © Joan Marie Arbogast
"Big Gulp" Copyright © Christine Armstrong
"All in the Family" Copyright © Becky Arnold
"Sticky Wealth" Copyright © Lisa Arnold
"Credit Confusion" Copyright © Jan Artrip
"Blackout" Copyright © Susan P. Ayers
"Freckles for Two" Copyright © Sandra Bacon
"Bird Eggs at Your Feet" and "Sidetracked" Copyright © Susanne Badilla
"Seek and Ye Shall Find" Copyright © Jill Baldwin
"Cloud Hopping" Copyright © Ellie Banas
"Starry Skies" Copyright © Shirley Bartone
"Fun, Fun, Fun" Copyright © Bonnie S. Baumgardner
"This Little Light" Copyright © Ann Beck
"Seeking Sanctuary" Copyright © Pierrette M. Begent
"Leopards in Church?" Copyright © Laurie Beithan
"Communion Confusion" Copyright © Melanie Bell
"Night-lite Reading" Copyright © Cheryl S. Bellocq
"Hound Cake" Copyright © Mary Belville
"Little Accountant" Copyright © Anne Marie Bennett
"Ask and Believe" Copyright © Sue Berry
"Cleanup Time" Copyright © Michelle Bianco
"Heart Antics" Copyright © Nancy Blackshear
"The Last Shall Be First" Copyright © Susan Blair
"At the End of Her Rope" and "Simple Joys" Copyright © Cathy Blake
"Out of Whack" Copyright © Gail Breach
"Cloudy Vision" Copyright © Renae Brobst
"Jack of All Trades" Copyright © Joan Brodie

ACKNOWLEDGMENTS

"Animal Activist" Copyright © Margaret M. Cuomo
"Full Moon" Copyright © Angie Curry
"Dessert Dynamo" Copyright © Carol B. Cuviello
"Substitute Story" Copyright © Joyce A. Davis
"The Extra Mile" Copyright © Vicki Davis
"Best Intentions" Copyright © Louise Day
"Holiday Hand-Me-Downs" Copyright © Alison Denight
"Pennies for His Thoughts" Copyright © Nancy Stoffregen Depa
"Brainstorm?" Copyright © Jennifer L. Diehl
"Map Reading 101" Copyright © Susan Dolle
"Sky-high Recycling" Copyright © Bambi Dossey
"Doing Time" Copyright © Chandra Drury
"No Room at the Inn" Copyright © Janine Dueck
"High Hopes" Copyright © Christy Duncan
"Gesundheit!" Copyright © Kim Duncan
"God on Call" Copyright © Carrie Duwe
"Loaded Question" Copyright © Kristy Roberts Dykes
"Driving Mr. Travis" Copyright © Jeannia Dykman
"Better Now?" Copyright © Flo Ege
"Strip Connections" Copyright © Elizabeth Eichenberger
"The Cheese Who Stands Alone" Copyright © Dawn Elgie
"Hearts Galore" Copyright © Beth Ellis
"Dingdong Praise" Copyright © Carmon S. Ellis
"Sweet Flavor" Copyright © Deanna Emmert
"Moo Testament" Copyright © Kathie Erwin
"Growing Feet" Copyright © Sharon Evans
"Kentucky Fried" Copyright © Cheryl K. Ewings
"Ham and Cheese on Rye" Copyright © Lynette Fasnacht
"Quirky Quartet" Copyright © Melba Ferrell
"Playing Church" Copyright © Roberta C. Fish
"Basket Baby" Copyright © Freda Fisk
"Name Nibblings" Copyright © Joyce Flakes
"Particular About Potatoes" Copyright © Margaret Flannery
"Spreading the Word" Copyright © Vera Ann Folden
"Hounds of Heaven" Copyright © Marcia Ford
"Variation on a Theme" Copyright © Brenda Fossum
"Countdown" Copyright © Dottie Free
"Accidents Do Happen" Copyright © Toni Friesen
"Little Lotto" and "Grown-up Wisdom" Copyright © Deana Galang

"Kid Genius," "Sassy Semantics," and "Waking Thought" Copyright © Kathy Gardaphé

"Chocolate Chortles" Copyright © Linda Garrison

"A Gift from God" Copyright © Amy Gaston

"Headaches and Heartaches" Copyright © Missy Gertz

"The Bread of Life" Copyright © Sandra Giffin

"Brotherly Love," "Frosting Fetish," and "Twinkle, Twinkle, Little Star" Copyright © Kathy Gnidovic

"Being Up Front" Copyright © Dori Goebel

"S-E-X" Copyright © Leanne Goff

"Thorny Thanks" Copyright © Jana Gorham

"A Child's Faith" Copyright © Christine Graham

"Petite Cheat" Copyright © Cheryl Graves

"Return to Sender" Copyright © Patti Greenman

"Journeying Mercies" Copyright © Darlene M. Grieco

"Free Admittance" Copyright © Betty Grigsby

"East of Eden" Copyright © Laura Groves

"Shower Surprise" Copyright © Kendra Halbert

"A No-Brainer" Copyright © Lynn Hall

"Going to See the King" Copyright © Sharon R. Hamatake

"A Mailbox in Heaven?" Copyright © Melissa Hamby

"Through the Roof" Copyright © Linda Hamilton

"Hot Rod to Heaven" Copyright © Debbie Hammers

"Prophet or Profit?" Copyright © Marilyn J. Hannay

"Learning Curve" Copyright © Jo-Ann M. Hansen

"Priceless Response" Copyright © Sandra Hanson

"All Is Calm" Copyright © Michelle Hardie

"Goats Tell It on the Mountain" Copyright © Debbie Harmon

"Factory Fun" Copyright © Debbie Harter

"Promises, Promises" Copyright © Phyllis Haughton

"Pull-Off Artist" Copyright © Sherrie Hawthorne

"A Lion in Sheep's Clothing" Copyright © Sally Edwards Hayes

"Sing It Again, James" Copyright © Barbara M. Heard

"Oh, Brother!" Copyright © Charlene Kay Heim

"Can You Keep a Secret?" Copyright © Tammy Heinrich

"Blonde Wishes" and "God in the Pew" Copyright © Kathleen Hicks

"Hallelujah Crazies" Copyright © Sharon Higgins

"Shirley Goodness" Copyright © Tamara Hill

"Spelling Stumper" Copyright © Tina Hill

"Take Me Out to the Ball Game" Copyright © Karen E. Hilverda
"Stuck in a Rut" Copyright © Connie Holman
"Tough Thursdays" Copyright © Sherry Holsted
"And God Bless . . ." Copyright © Virginia Kelly Homan
"In Jesus' Lap" Copyright © Ginger Horn
"Extra Credit" Copyright © Jolene Horn
"The Big Nursery" Copyright © Tamara Hough
"The Greenhouse Effect" Copyright © Rhonda Hover
"Yankee Doodle Dandy" Copyright © Rita Howard
"Mint?" Copyright © Jean Hudson
"For Men Only" Copyright © Beth Hugdahl
"Happy Hello" Copyright © Ruth Hultgren
"It Keeps Going . . . and Going" Copyright © Frances J. Hutson
"Heart Check" Copyright © Jeanette Hyatt
"Grin and Bear It" Copyright © Kirsten Jackson
"Batteries Not Included" Copyright © Lois Hutcherson Jackson
"In a Class by Himself" Copyright © Ruth F. Jacobs
"A Plateful of Prayer?" Copyright © Diana L. James
"Time Out" Copyright © Donna R. James
"Sounding Off" Copyright © Sandra James
"The Golden Rule" Copyright © Linda LaMar Jewell
"Bear with Me" Copyright © Carol Johnson
"Beddy Bye," "Boy and Girl Bugs," and "Mixed Apology" Copyright © Daniella Johnson
"Fishy Funny" Copyright © Kristen Johnson
"Fruit of the Spirit" Copyright © Maria Johnson
"Fact of Origin" Copyright © Sally Johnson
"Eye in the Sky" Copyright © Yvette Johnson
"Birthday Invitation" Copyright © Marion L. Jones
"Disciples Expanded" Copyright © Nena Jurek
"Scripture Mix-up" Copyright © Marjory Kasen
"A Word to the Wise" Copyright © Bambi L. Kelly
"Runaway Emotions" Copyright © Kelly Kennard
"Oh, Brother!" Copyright © Terri E. Kesterke
"Anybody Home?" Copyright © Karen Ketzler
"Ready and Waiting" Copyright © Peggy Key
"Pulled It Off Single-handedly" Copyright © Mrs. Harvey Kidd
"Udderly Confused" Copyright © Kelly A. Kim
"A Higher Order" Copyright © Susan C. Kimber

"Wedding Bell Blues" Copyright © Doris Marie Mataya
"Special Needs" Copyright © Debi Matzke
"Scripture Shorts" Copyright © Martha Matzke
"The Other Abe" Copyright © Annelle Maurer
"Breath of God" Copyright © Billie Mazzei
"The Great Escape" Copyright © Rhonda Meadows
"Mary and Larry" Copyright © Autumn D. Meinardus
"No Bones About It" Copyright © Rhonda Mendoza
"Trouble in the Ranks" Copyright © M. Joan Miller
"Vegetarian Surprise" Copyright © Melanie Miller
"Which Mary?" Copyright © Valerie Miller
"Come On Along" Copyright © Tina Mitchell
"Armor of God" Copyright © Colleen Monaghan
"Disney Missionary" Copyright © Jan Mullaney
"Call It!" Copyright © Kay Murphree
"What He Said" Copyright © M. Doris Murphy
"Maternal Malpractice" Copyright © Elise Nacion
"Womb Activity" Copyright © Barbara Neale
"Have a Lick" Copyright © Danielle Nelson
"Double-Checking" Copyright © Nora Newport
"Special Request" Copyright © Gladys Noble
"Customer Service" Copyright © Kimberly Noel
"U Turn" Copyright © Lou Ann Noren
"Creative Bowling" Copyright © Linda Nutell
"'Handy' Capped" Copyright © Lori Beezhold O'Dea
"How Romantic" Copyright © Kyongmi Odell
"Be Still, My Heart" Copyright © Christine O'Donnell
"Joy to the World" Copyright © Robin Oppenhuizen
"Diet Doldrums" Copyright © Michelle A. Pablo
"Here Comes the Bride" Copyright © Robin Kendle Parker
"Shouting the Commandments" Copyright © Katie Payne
"A Call Away" Copyright © Laura Ament Peck
"Whose House?" Copyright © Stacy Penalva
"Play Ball!" Copyright © Taffy Pfaehler
"A Real Live Nativity" Copyright © Lisa I. Poole
"A Twisted Commandment" Copyright © Eric and Jayne Post
"Mouthing Off" Copyright © Helen Prater
"A Big Surprise" Copyright © Patricia Puckett
"Me Too!" Copyright © Frances Pullen

"Spirited Reply" Copyright © Tammie Quesenberry
"Fiery Fracas" Copyright © Shelly Rankin
"Passing Acquaintance" Copyright © Elsie Ratowski
"Bedtime Priorities" Copyright © Kim Reade
"Intestinal Interest" Copyright © Sharon Redd
"Frosty Effects" Copyright © Ann Skodje Redding
"Time Tales" Copyright © Shirley Redmond
"Give Us Lord Our Jelly Bread" Copyright © Brenda L. Reed
"Last Isn't the End" Copyright © Ginger Reed
"Solid Rock" Copyright © Linda Reed
"Liberty and Justice for All" Copyright © Rhonda Reese
"Black and Blue" Copyright © Lori Richards
"How Do You Spell Belief?" Copyright © Kathy Richardson
"Hard Sell" Copyright © Janet Riehecky
"Bible Vegetables" Copyright © Dolores Ritter
"Landlubber" Copyright © Lynn M. Roberts
"Uh-oh!" Copyright © Terrie Rodgers
"Storybook End" Copyright © Carrie Roemmich
"Material World" Copyright © Linda Rogalski
"A Fistful of 'Daniel-lions'" Copyright © Deana Rogers
"Banana Nana" Copyright © Kristal Rogers
"Genetics Guess" Copyright © Debra L. Rokicki
"Fishy Tale" Copyright © Carol Rose
"Taking Charge" Copyright © Pamela Rubeo
"First Things First" Copyright © Dawn Ryan
"Better Check . . ." Copyright © Suzy Ryan
"The Hole Truth" Copyright © Arlene Sampson
"Pint-Sized Bargain Hunter" Copyright © Aleene Sanders
"Wet Wish" Copyright © Donna Sapienza
"To Dye For" Copyright © Teresa Saueressig
"King of the Jewels" Copyright © Lee A. Schedler
"Cleaning Crew" and "Out of the Mouths of Babes" Copyright © Jane Schmidt
"What Kind of Christian?" Copyright © Connie Schmotzer
"Junior Revelation" Copyright © Robin Searles
"Tagged in Heaven" Copyright © Donna Seller
"Howard Be Thy Father" Copyright © Fran Severance
"A Plant for Life" Copyright © Samantha Sfirlea
"Night Vision" Copyright © Penny L. Shemory

ACKNOWLEDGMENTS

"He's Got Me Covered" Copyright © Kim Sherer
"Persistent Person" Copyright © Sherry Shiffler
"A Still, Small Voice" Copyright © Dayle A. Shockley
"Mind Games" Copyright © Orla C. Shup
"Walking Sermon" Copyright © Helen Siml
"Good News for Presbyterians" Copyright © Susan Simmons
"Lettuce Talk" Copyright © Mary H. Simpson
"Home on the Range?" "I Got Brains!" and "Seed of a Different Kind" Copyright © Lisa Skaggs
"The Cola Wars" Copyright © Ruth Skar
"High Flying" Copyright © Becky Smith
"Hail Excitement" Copyright © Donna C. Smith
"Mary Who?" Copyright © Diane Spicer
"May Eye Help You?" Copyright © Cheryl Spinks
"Knock, Knock" Copyright © Linda K. Sproull
"Movin' On Up" Copyright © Barbara Spurlock
"Mighty Maker" Copyright © Brenda Stearns
"Crafty Speller" Copyright © Kelly Steffen
"Please, Mr. Please" Copyright © Karen M. Stevenson
"Joy on the Journey" and "Logical Extension" Copyright © Cheryl Stewart
"A Kinder Punishment" and "Maid in Heaven" Copyright © Michelle Stewart
"Whisker Philosophy" Copyright © Darlene Stiefel
"King of the Car" Copyright © Maxine Stout
"Rural Shopping" Copyright © Marilyn Stroup
"Teeter Totter" Copyright © Cynthia Sturtz
"A Different Kind of Amen" Copyright © Willette Swanson
"Quick Learner" Copyright © Tambi Swiney
"Nesting Instincts" Copyright © Carla Talley
"Prickly Peas" Copyright © Julie Taylor
"Divine Direction" Copyright © Pegi Tehan
"The Eleventh Commandment" Copyright © Shelley Telfer
"Pretty Cheesy" Copyright © Ardith Thiel
"Just Helping Out" Copyright © Diane Thom
"Wild Thing" Copyright © Audrey Thomas
"Important Guest" Copyright © Rachel Thomas
"Mr. Donuthead" Copyright © Teresia Gravley Thomason
"Family Mix-up" Copyright © Paulette Thompson

Moody Press, a ministry of Moody Bible Institute,
is designed for education, evangelization, and edification.
If we may assist you in knowing more about Christ
and the Christian life, please write us without obligation:
Moody Press, c/o MLM, Chicago, Illinois 60610.